Home Bible Studies

The great merit of this book is that it is written out of practical experience. Dr. Copley and his wife saw the tremendous spiritual need of their neighbours all round them in a housing development, and wanted to help them. But "going to church" was out of the question. For one thing it was miles away and for another, well it was something you just did not do.

So Dr. Copley and his wife began by asking neighbours to a Home Bible Study in their own new house.

And they came! And it worked!

The Home Bible Study Group movement has now proved that this kind of activity by ordinary folk without any special training can be a tremendous power in the hearts and homes of other ordinary folk, and this book tells how it can be done.

TITLES IN THIS SERIES:

HOME BIBLE STUDIES

Forming and Running an Adult Group

by **DEREK B. COPLEY, Ph.D.**

Principal, Moorlands Bible College

EXETER:
THE PATERNOSTER PRESS

ISBN: 0 85364 126 9
Copyright © 1972 The Paternoster Press

AUSTRALIA:
Emu Book Agencies Pty., Ltd.,
1 Lee Street, Sydney, N.S.W.

SOUTH AFRICA:
Oxford University Press
P.O. Box 1141, Oxford House,
11 Buitencingle Street, Cape Town

Made and Printed in Great Britain for
The Paternoster Press Paternoster House
3 Mount Radford Crescent Exeter Devon
by Maslands Limited
Fore Street Tiverton Devon

Contents

Contents

Preface

FOR SEVERAL YEARS my wife and I have been involved in Home Bible Studies both in Britain and the U.S.A. On many occasions when I have been speaking about home evangelism, Christians have requested copies of Bible study material which we used. The Appendix contains notes that have formed the basis of such Bible studies, together with a list of useful books.

This book is intended for members of groups which meet regularly and who need help in selecting and preparing passages and material for an extended course of studies. Bible studies for students and young people have been held in homes for many years but only recently has adult work of a similar nature become a major means of evangelism and teaching. This book is limited to this type of work in order to help those who are already involved in it or who want to know how to make a start. We hope that readers who have so far been apprehensive about starting a Home Bible Study will be sufficiently encouraged to begin one in their own home.

Although we have attempted to deal with detailed strategy of participation and leadership, it should not be thought that this is merely a manual, for we have included many personal experiences and some of the successes and failures of our work. We have included as much practical information as possible to show how difficulties have been overcome and how individual lives have been changed by group study.

One

Why Home Bible Studies?

IT IS NOT EASY TO FIND REASONS FOR THE SUCCESS OF Bible studies and other meetings in homes. I believe the blessing is very much linked to the changing way of life in the West because the home can cater for people who are caught up in this rapid change. We live in a nation which regards church attendance as socially and spiritually unnecessary. In fact, the image presented by the visible church seems to most people to be unreal and irrelevant, unconcerned with them as individuals. Life has become so impersonal that many people cannot say with any certainty that they have any genuine friends. Even unbelievers are beginning to agree that future prospects of happiness are bleak indeed. It has been said recently that although our living standards are rising the quality of life is steadily decreasing.

From my contacts over the past few years, it is abundantly clear that there are many who could be helped in their search for the truth by those who are prepared to make an effort to understand and be a real friend to those sincerely seeking the answers to life's questions. Simply to preach the gospel in a formal way and leave it at that seems a mockery to so many people. They also need someone in whom they can trust and confide, whom they can regard as an authority because of his or her God-given wisdom.

Offering ourselves and our homes to those in need of spiritual and physical help is one way of showing them that God is real and that Christianity is relevant. The home is a natural setting for relaxed conversation and for getting to grips with my neighbour's problems. He may be shy about coming to church since it lies completely outside his own experience, but comfortably seated in a living room he is content even to have an open Bible on his lap. You may think that your neighbours are not the kind of people who would come to a Bible study. So did we until we tried it! I suspect that most of the embarrassment is on our side!

To show that God does use home Bible studies as an effective means of witness we have included a few stories here, true in every respect except that the names of the people have been changed. They begin with accounts of how several people came to realise their need of Jesus Christ through studying the Bible in a home, and finish with stories of Christians whose lives and witness were dramatically changed through their participation in home Bible studies.

Much Time to Make Up

Jack and Edith lived in a 3-storey rambling Victorian house in a suburb of Manchester. Though he was in his fifties and she in her forties they had two small children aged 3 and 2. Their conversion was brought about by a series of contacts with various people. Edith was desperately lonely though she was surrounded by houses and people. On one occasion when she'd been housebound for several weeks because the children had measles she sent a note to the nursery-school teacher asking her to call in for coffee and a chat. She had heard that this teacher was "religious".

As a result she received an invitation to come to a Young Wives' Bible Study which she found interesting and different from anything she had ever attended. On the nights when Edith went to the study one of the husbands used to go and keep Jack company. Frequently they said nothing about Christianity or the Bible. They simply watched television with him and talked generally trying to get to know him as a friend. After many weeks of Bible studies Edith came to a realisation that her life up to that point had been a real mess and she asked the Lord Jesus to take over her life.

She was so absolutely thrilled by what had happened and by what she was learning about the Lord through the Bible studies that she rushed home after each meeting and told Jack every detail. She made him look up the passages with her and explained them to him with a genuine childlike excitement. Soon, he too was ready to commit himself to Christ as his wife had done.

Adjusting to a new life after many years of the old ways was both interesting and amusing for them. Now they had Bible studies to go to and they didn't want to miss a single one. Off they would rush to the launderette in the evening, put the clothes in to wash and dash next door to the pub for a drink. Back they'd go to the launderette to collect the clothes and off to the Bible study! But soon they found that the visit to the pub became less interesting and they simply stopped going.

Jack and Edith grew rapidly in the Christian faith and when they moved away to Scotland after a year of attending a home Bible study they went earnestly desiring to tell others about their new-found faith. They started a Bible study in their home and brought a blessing to many in their village.

Music Through the Walls

Our group was singing carols just before Christmas and our neighbour Mary was listening to the joyful sound floating through the wall. She longed to join that happy crowd of people who met each week for Bible study, yet she lacked the courage to join us. But one day she did come, and that began a twelve-month struggle as God sought to come into her life. Somehow she knew that she should accept Christ as Saviour yet she could not face the decision. About this time David Watson was conducting a mission at Manchester University and I had been asked to serve as an assistant missioner. Mary accepted an invitation from my wife to attend the first meeting of the mission, and then followed the second and the third. Each night Mary was there and finally at the end of the week when an appeal was made she joined the many who had already made a decision for Christ.

A Soldier Joins God's Army

One day, David, a teenage soldier on leave, was brought to our Bible study by some Christian friends. For many years his invalid mother had prayed for his conversion yet he had no interest in God. Quietly yet definitely God worked in his heart during that one hour with the Bible and after the meeting was over he entered into earnest conversation with Joe, an older Christian. That night Joe's warmth and personality radiated the love of Christ and we prayed that there would be a real breakthrough in David's life. So far as we knew nothing had happened and we said goodbye to him and wished him a safe journey back to his barracks. Next week our Christian friends were bubbling over with excitement as they reported to us that David had told them on the way home that during his conversation with Joe he has given his life to Christ; yet Joe had no idea that anything had happened while he talked to David.

A P.C. is Arrested

Peter was a police constable in a tough area of Manchester and had been brought up in the Roman Catholic Church. Like many Catholics he possessed an RSV Bible yet he didn't understand its message. Although he lived ten miles away, he had heard about our Bible studies and began to come regularly. His main problem was that he was often on night duty immediately following the meeting which necessitated his coming complete with uniform, helmet and truncheon, a rare sight at a Bible study! In spite of his tough appearance he had many vital questions in his mind about Christianity, and he began to see that the answers could be found by reading the Bible. He slowly realised that he needed to trust Christ as the all-sufficient Saviour and in a quiet way his heart was opened to Jesus. Things did not go well for him after this and he experienced some severe personal trials, yet he was able to face and overcome them in the strength that Christ gives.

Is There Really Life After Death?

Mrs. Smith had recently lost her husband. As she thought about his death she grew anxious about life-after-death. Mrs. Smith decided to seek advice from her church but received very little help. During the course of the year we used to ask members of the group for their suggestions of subjects or passages which they would like to study. Mrs. Smith had still not discovered the answers to her questions and requested a study on the after-life. As we opened the Bible and read the relevant verses it all became clear and for the first time since her husband's death she experienced real peace of mind, and gradually as the months went by, her confidence in God increased.

How Clear the Bible is Now!

Jim had heard the Gospel many times at school yet in those formative years he had not seen the reality of Christianity. Our first contact with him was the result of a hole in the fence between his house and ours, through which we used to borrow gardening equipment from each other. The hole was eventually boarded up, but Jim became a regular member of our group, and so did his wife. Soon the childhood memories of Bible stories and verses returned and Jim knew that God was calling him to rededicate his life to Jesus Christ. Some time later he told us that his new awareness of the truths found in the Bible was like scales falling from his eyes!

What Are You Thinking?

The blessings of home Bible studies are not limited to introducing members to Jesus Christ. Couples are sometimes introduced to each other and then romance comes along! An unusual story which began round our fireside that is of Mark and Elizabeth. Mark had been coming for several months, bringing with him a number of friends, including a young lady called Elizabeth. On one particular evening none of the friends was able to come except Elizabeth. On the way home from the study he suddenly stopped the car and became engrossed in thought, which seemed to Elizabeth a strange thing to do. When she asked him what he was thinking he replied rather casually, "I was wondering if you wanted to marry me."

As it seemed rather a tentative suggestion she enquired "Do you love me?"

"I'm not sure but I think that I could grow into loving you," said Mark.

And so he did. From this strange encounter developed a marriage, and now together Mark and Elizabeth witness for Christ.

The Biblical Basis of Home Evangelism

Much has been written in other books about the specific area of home evangelism and I do not think it necessary to repeat what they have said. It is sufficient to notice that the Lord Himself and His disciples frequently used people's homes as a setting in which to preach the good news. It is also true that the early church made use of the home for many of its activities.

There is no chapter-and-verse instruction as to the

detailed strategy of evangelism in this year or any other year. One of my students recently prepared a thesis on "The pattern of evangelism in the early church." After working on it for several weeks he came to tell me that he had been unable to discover any distinct form of strategy stated by the Bible relating to evangelism. This indicates that even in those days God did not limit Himself to a rigid way of working. And if we read the history of the church up to the present day it becomes obvious that His blessing rests not just upon those who are content with established routines of evangelism, but especially upon those who involve themselves in what He is doing in less usual and sometimes more effective ways.

There are many types of evangelism ranging from Sunday School work to coffee bar witnessing for which we have no direct command from Scripture, except that God expects us to evangelise. If God is using a particular way of reaching people and that way does not violate what the Bible teaches, then we must conclude that it is of the Lord. Home evangelism is an example of this. All over the Western world homes are being turned into centres of activity where people may come to learn about Christianity and be introduced to Christ. Bible studies in the home form only a very small part of the many different types of outreach work going on in the living rooms of God's people today, although it is beyond the scope of this book to deal with the other methods.

In many areas where Churches have held gospel efforts in their own buildings and failed to make an impact on the outsider, meetings in homes have successfully reached people who are really concerned but are untouched by institutional routine. I suppose that in Churches such as these, it is easy for the congregations to drift unwittingly into a state in which they imagine the seventies are going to be fruitless years for the Church and are resigned to accepting the situation. It may be necessary for many

Churches to reorientate their thinking on evangelism. Using the home is not a new idea but because of the effectiveness in reaching non-believers, responsible Christians are taking a more careful look at this means of evangelism.

Pioneer Evangelism via the Home

There are many residential areas where the Christians are forced to travel several miles to other churches simply because there is no local evangelical fellowship to attend. Often those Christians are led by the Lord into pioneer work where they live, setting up a home study group and reaching their neighbours through this means. There are many instances of fellowships which had their beginnings in home study groups. The warmth and genuine interest shown by the Christians tends to draw unbelievers into the home and into a personal relationship with the Lord. Although this would necessitate doing less work in their own churches, any church with the slightest evangelistic zeal should heartily commend its members to this work. There may even be the situation in which there is only one Christian family in a locality but this need not be a barrier to winning their neighbours for Christ by using their home.

A word of caution should be said here about splinter groups. These often arise through members of local churches becoming dissatisfied, which results in their meeting exclusively in a home and never with the fellowship to which they belong. The normal function of a Home Bible Study Group is to feed Christians into the local church or to become the foundation for such a church in an area where there is no evangelical witness. There are many problems in helping young Christians to integrate into church fellowships but nevertheless the groups should seek to establish the Christians in a suitable local church.

We should not forget that churches are responsible to evangelise those living near the church building. There is no reason why the home should not be used to supplement or even replace special gospel efforts. Again, many central church Bible studies, if such are held, are badly attended, and therefore ineffective, indeed irrelevant. To replace these by several simultaneous home Bible studies frequently results in a three-fold or even five-fold increase in people studying the Bible. There are few fellowships which can honestly say that they are satisfied with the proportion of members actively studying the Scriptures, so that any means used to promote more attention to God's Word must surely bring glory to God.

The Scope of Home Bible Studies

It is quite natural for people of similar interests to enjoy being together informally. Organisations selling various products rely on housewives being able to invite a few friends to their house to see their product with a view to a sale. Home studies can often be quite normal and relaxed when friends get together, since it is not too big a step to go from social conversation to spending a while talking about the Bible.

Ladies' groups often meet over coffee in the mornings or tea in the afternoons. Young Wives' Groups usually meet during the evening and often combine a Bible study with a cookery demonstration or a talk on home safety. Bachelor girls enjoy each other's company and can be a means of reaching others in a similar situation. My wife has been involved in a "Pram Club" in which mothers of young children met for a short study while one member looked after the children, usually done on a rota basis. Students can reach their fellow undergraduates by organising a Bible study.

As you can see from these different types of groups, wherever there is a possibility of personal friends and contacts getting together, there is an opportunity to introduce others to Jesus Christ, and to help the Christians seek a deeper relationship with their Saviour. In Romans 10:17 we read that "faith cometh by hearing, and hearing by the Word of God." If by any means we can persuade others to sincerely read and study their Bibles then faith will surely spring up and cause them to commit their lives to Christ. The power of God's Word has not changed, we can still expect to see miracles when the Word takes root in men's hearts.

Two

Finding People to Come

I SUPPOSE IT IS FAR EASIER TO LOOK BACK AND SEE HOW readily our own Home Bible Studies began than it is to advise those who believe that God is calling them to open their homes. We began to make plans as soon as the Lord gave us the firm conviction that it was His will and after that everything seemed to fit into place. As we mentioned in the previous chapter, such studies are appropriate both in a spiritually barren area or where the local church believes that this way of evangelism and teaching would complement its own outreach activities in that locality.

We lived in an area devoid of a vital Christian Church and yet there were literally dozens of Christians living there who travelled to Churches in other districts. We felt that things would be so much easier if other local believers could catch the vision we had for home evangelism and yet had there been no available support I have no doubt the Lord would have shown us how to begin alone.

Having met several local Christians it was a relatively easy task to compile a list of names and addresses of most believers in the locality. We decided that the best way to present our plans to them was to send each one a letter outlining what we had in mind, inviting them to come to an informal meeting in our home to hear what we had to say. Only a small number came but the vision that God had given us became their burden too and several people agreed to help us. No doubt where a local Church is using

19

home evangelism in its own area a similar meeting could be arranged for those belonging to that particular Church.

Before anyone can be invited to a study there are a number of decisions to be made such as the place and time of meeting, who is going to lead the first and subsequent studies and the strategy with which other people are to be drawn into the group. It would be fair to say that the Christians who have had a burden from the Lord for the work and who have taken the initiative should bear much of the responsibility at this stage.

There is a diversity of opinion as to how often a group should meet and the decision about this should take into consideration the needs of the area and the availability of those who form the nucleus of the group. Many home studies are arranged on a weekly basis, as ours was, while others prefer to meet only once a fortnight or once a month. We decided on a weekly study because our neighbours were the kind of people who did not find it too difficult to be free almost every week on a given night and it was not long before they made a routine of being free each Wednesday.

There is nothing special about Wednesday except that after weighing all the pros and cons of the different nights this particular one caused the least inconvenience. It is impossible to choose a night which doesn't exclude someone in the group and in the end one has to be as understanding and tactful as possible when it comes to the choice.

Choosing the time to begin the study is again a matter of a compromise between various extremes. There will be those who have to put children to bed or who work late, for whom 7.30 p.m. would be too early, and to finish much later than 9 p.m. might exclude those who must get up early next morning for work or who have baby-sitters to consider. So, we decided on a one hour meeting from 8 p.m. until 9 p.m.

It is often very inconvenient to the hosts to have the meetings at the same house each week as it causes a perpetual upheaval which is rather tiresome after several months. On the other hand, considerable confusion can arise where the group goes to a different house each week, especially where a number of members come irregularly and may not find out where the meeting is to be held through missing one or two studies. One way of avoiding this problem would be to plan the list of hosts well in advance and to circulate the list among the members. An alternative to rotating each week is to have the meetings at one house for a period of time, say three months, then change to another one. In this way the inconvenience is shared between several people. We always held the studies at our house because we felt that many adults prefer some kind of routine and feel more at ease in the same surroundings each week. At first it took rather a long time to set up the room for each study but eventually we hardly noticed the work and took it in our stride. Even holidays, hospitalization, and the birth of our first child did not prevent the weekly meetings being held in our home; we simply passed on the responsibility of leadership to other members at these times.

Assuming that you have made as many plans as you can and are either working with a nucleus of Christians or even alone, there remains the task of finding people to come. If the study is intended to be very local involving mostly those within a short distance then the reaction to invitations may depend on our own reputation among our neighbours, in the local shops, etc. We should ask ourselves what they really think of us. Do they see us as normal people with normal interests in life who happen to do a lot of Christian and social work? Or do they view us as being rather odd and isolated from the real world, possibly even fanatically religious?

A Christian need not go to the extreme of indulging in

everything that worldly people do in order to show that he is a normal person, but I do believe that the Christian who has isolated himself from society will find it difficult to persuade people to attend a Bible study, simply because he may give the impression that Christianity is isolationism. Of course, we must not tolerate evil or be associated with anything which is ungodly but this does not preclude personal contact with unbelievers. I knew a Christian whose only contact with his neighbours was the pushing of tracts through their letter-box from time to time!

Ladies probably have more opportunity to get to know their neighbours than do the men, and even then it may take some time for their confidence in us as people to be sufficient to merit inviting them to study the Bible with us. One of the criticisms which the Lord made of the disciples of His day was that the unbelievers were far more thorough in their secular pursuits than the disciples were in the propagation of the Gospel (Luke 16: 8). If an unbeliever seeks wealth and fame he will go to any extreme to fulfil his desire. How much more effort should we make when what we are trying to do has eternal value. It may be necessary to take up some new interest in order to have some common ground with our neighbours and to show that we are really quite normal after all.

In Ch. 6 I have written about pastoral care of members of the group in which we may have a responsibility. I think that Christians have spent so much time talking about salvation by faith that they think that good works are simply something which unbelievers do in order to merit salvation. Not forgetting the sovereign work of God, half the secret of having people accept our invitations lies in their seeing that our faith results in good works. It is clearly up to each Christian to decide in what way they can influence people for the Lord and bring them into contact with the living Word. Some may have the liberty to become members of such things as golf clubs or the W.V.S. in order to be in contact with people; some others may believe that this would be wrong and would constitute "loving the world."

Having lived in the area for only a few months, we had the advantage that people had not yet built up their personal prejudices about us and at the same time we had taken every opportunity to make contact with them. We didn't invite neighbours indiscriminately but restricted our invitations to those who knew us. For instance, when we were visiting one young couple, the husband happened to make a chance remark that some years ago he used to enjoy listening to keen Christians discussing the Scriptures. We remembered what he had said and after some months invited him and his wife to our home for Bible Study. They accepted, and more than a year later were still faithful members of the group. Other local people accepted our invitations because they were unable to attend church regularly due to ill health and the travel involved. There were those who had experienced personal tragedies who felt that through studying the Bible they would find real help. Quite a number of Christians, young in the faith, decided to come because their own churches had no meeting in which they could actively participate in discussion of the Bible. Some came because they felt lost and inadequate in much larger church groups and had never really grown spiritually since their conversion. One young housewife had a most unusual motive for wanting to come—she had no personal knowledge of God or His Word but desired to tell her growing child about the true Christian faith.

Some Christians who open their homes for Bible study are disappointed when the only ones who come at first are believers. Our own first meeting consisted solely of Christians, which is what we had expected to some degree. I had prepared a study called "The World in Need" in which we discussed the necessity of faith in Christ if life was to have any real meaning. At this meeting many of the Christians realised that they had a responsibility to invite their friends to come and study the Bible.

If at any stage before opening our home we were anxious about whether people would come, we need not have been. The one or two neighbours who came for the first few weeks visited their own friends to tell them about the studies and it simply snowballed from there onwards. We even stopped advertising special topics in the newspaper which we had done for the first few months. Within a year the group grew excessively large both from the discussion point of view and because our poor little four-by-three-yards living room simply wasn't big enough. At one point we had some thirty adults squeezed into the room, and it was then that we realised that such a crowd was not conducive to good study, and after praying about it we tactfully and privately suggested that some of the more mature Christians should absent themselves occasionally, though not *all* on the same day!

Although we were always thrilled to see a good crowd of people, the most profitable discussions took place when there were eight or ten people present. In Ch. 5 I have emphasised how essential it is to make people feel at home so that they will be studying the Bible in a completely natural atmosphere. When we invite a few friends round for a chat we normally wouldn't dream of having more than ten, otherwise the occasion would become too crowded and formal. Because we attend churches where large crowds gather to hear the Word expounded I think we have probably been influenced in our thinking to such an extent that we cannot imagine how God can bless half-a-dozen people in our living room. In fact when a group has more than a dozen people attending regularly the leader should consider the formation of a second group by splitting up the original one. Prior to doing this it is clear that there should be someone in the group who could be the leader of the other group.

You may imagine that there were no disappointments in finding people to come. There were many, especially when those who came only once or twice never returned. There was one night during the first month of meetings when only two people came, making four in all, but even then we had a profitable time. Some too professed conversion and yet seemed to lose interest after a few weeks. But the failures were more than balanced by the ones who grew spiritually from being babes in Christ and those whose conversion experience was a lasting one.

Three

Getting the Programme Together

L ET US SAY THAT YOU HAVE DECIDED TO HAVE A HOME
Bible study group and have discussed your plans
and aims with a few Christian friends. You have decided
on a night, and have taken the plunge of inviting non-
Christian friends and neighbours and you are now faced
with the question, "What do we discuss?"

Some groups decide on the night itself what they shall
study, others plough through an Old Testament book over
a period of two years or more. Our experience has shown
us that God blesses a well-thought-out programme which
takes into consideration the needs of the group. For
example, to throw your non-Christian neighbour into a
deep theological discussion on a lengthy passage from
Daniel is the best way to ensure that he never comes again.
But a discussion on "Why should we pray?" or "What
is a Christian?" may well answer questions he has been
harbouring in his mind for some time.

One must, therefore, be sensitive to the people in the
group in planning a programme. The basic aims of the
group must constantly be remembered, namely to win
friends and neighbours to Christ and to draw Christians
who are young in the faith into a closer relationship with
their Saviour. As the group develops then obviously one's

programmes will change from basic topics into slightly deeper or wider-ranging topics, Scripture passages, specific doctrinal truths, and difficult prophecies.

A home Bible Study Group which is successful seems to move through several stages of spiritual growth: the Young Group, the Growing Group, and the Mature Group. By these headings I don't mean young or mature in age but in the spiritual understanding which comes as a group studies the Scriptures together. I will discuss each stage showing how the group may develop in its longing for spiritual food. I have given examples of topics and Scripture passages which seem suitable to the group at each stage of its growth. However, this does not mean that the young group should not move into a heavy topic if it so desires, or that the mature group should not deal with basic points in the Christian faith. The discussion in the young group would of necessity be on a shallower level whereas the mature group could talk about the simpler areas of the Christian faith with greater insight.

(A) *The Young Group*

It is very often best to start with nothing but a full programme of carefully chosen topics for a new or young group, although the group should before very long, progress from topical studies to studying the Bible passages in sequence, as God caused it to be written. Even though some of the members may well be quite mature Christians they should not mind discussing basic topics in a way which will help non-believers to see the Christian point of view as expressed in the Bible.

Here is a possible series of studies for a new group:
The world in need.
The necessity of the Cross.
Where are the Prophets today?
What is a Christian?
Is the Bible historically and spiritually inspired?

The meaning of the Resurrection.
The Bible in my life.
Why should we pray?
Should we worry?
Miracles.

You may well get some friends to your studies who have no knowledge of the Scriptures at all or worse still a little knowledge that is quite inaccurate. Topics are a marvellous way of bringing out truths from the Scriptures in an easily digestible form. For example, the many references in Scripture to good works, faith, heaven and sin etc. can be brought out in the discussion and applied to our own lives under the topic "What is a Christian?"

However, one must be true to the Scriptures and not choose topics which the Bible doesn't really deal with. For example, euthanasia and abortion though interesting and important do not lend themselves to a proper Bible study because Scripture does not deal with them *as such*. One must beware of choosing topics which would give rise to intellectual football instead of practical, searching, Bible study.

In choosing titles for the topics one must be careful to avoid theological terms or evangelical jargon. For example, if the topic under discussion is "The Rapture" it will mean more to Christians and non-Christians alike if you simply call it "How Christ will take us to Heaven." In studying the Genesis flood it may be best to call it "Did Noah's Ark really exist?" Sometimes we are so steeped in jargon that we find it difficult to simplify our terms or realise that outsiders may not understand our meanings. Our topic headings must be an exercise in public relations whereby we attract people and make them feel able to cope with the discussion.

If the leader himself feels either inexperienced or unable to cope with preparing the details of his studies from scratch he may wish to make use of the many Bible Study courses now in print and available from many Churches, bookshops and Christian literature distributors. The reader may obtain some ideas of useful books by referring to the book list in the Appendix. It would do no harm to buy some of these simply to get ideas from them. However, the Scriptures must take supreme importance in our discussion, and where these Bible helps actually do help to clarify and simplify they are fine. If they take the place of actually looking at and studying the Scripture then they should not be used. Our aim is to see what God says through His Word not to see what other men's opinions are on the subject.

(B) *The Growing Group*

One of the remarkable things about a regular study of the Bible is that those whose hearts are open to the work of the Holy Spirit soon develop a hungering and thirsting after spiritual food. This, of course, should be our aim and earnest prayer. My own lack of faith has been evident when I was surprised by suggestions that were made for deeper studies.

Some members delight in suggesting topics which even the best leader could not handle. If this happens the leader may just as well admit that an expert ought to be called in to lead that particular study. One person in our group suggested a bird's eye view of the whole of the Book of Revelation in one study! I called in a friend who was especially knowledgeable on that book and who happened to be a teacher as well. He went hard at it for fifty minutes with everyone either taking notes or sitting enthralled. It was a memorable evening and very helpful in giving background for future detailed studies from that book.

To ask the group to make suggestions for future studies and then pause while the ideas flow is hopeless. People just will not suggest topics while everyone else is listening. It is more profitable to ask for ideas from people while you chat with them informally after the study. People open up more over a cup of tea and when they think no one is overhearing their "silly suggestions". We often found that people would pop in the next day and hand us a piece of paper with some ideas on it or even stop my wife in the supermarket and suggest some thoughts.

For example, as the group grew spiritually they wanted some studies on Free Will; What is the Real Church?; The Inspiration and Authority of the Bible (we used a visiting American professor of Theology for that one); the book of James in five studies; Knowing for Sure; the Problem of Pain; Satan, does he exist?; How does God guide us?, and many more. The ideas became exciting and the studies lively and full of real practical help in the Christian life. During this "growing stage" the group increased to thirty on some nights—quite a squash in a small living room. There was a flux of new faces mingled with those who usually attended and this meant that the studies had to cater for their needs as well as those who were making real progress in the faith. The Gospel inevitably came out, usually through someone's warm, uncalculated testimony somewhere in the discussion time. We were thrilled to see the effect of these discussions on the lives of those who had never heard the Bible discussed so meaningfully and personally. They continued to come and in several cases we saw their lives changed by the Holy Spirit using the Bible and Christians together in our home.

Frequently in the midst of a lively discussion ideas for future studies would pop out all over the place. While studying Forgiveness, the question of the next life would come up. This would be suggested as a separate study since time would not allow for two such huge topics in a one hour's study. During a discussion on the functions of the members of a local church, the whole question of women keeping silence might spring up. This can be quite a study in itself especially in a Home Bible Study group where the women are encouraged to be anything but silent.

It is just good psychology to ask people for their ideas. It makes them feel wanted and valued. Also better than asking "What do *you* want to study?" I found "What shall *we* study?" more apt to draw people into feeling a part of the group. If the group is made up of both Christians and non-believers then you will no doubt receive suggestions from both. It is obviously right to accept a non-believer's suggestions of topics. It is for them that we instituted these studies and we should try to encourage them. Obviously where any awkward suggestions are made, the leader must deal tactfully and carefully while remaining true to the Scriptures.

(C) *The Established Group*

After six months or a year the leader will be able to recognise that several members have made really good spiritual progress and need both the chance to study consecutive passages of Scripture and extra responsibility within the group.

The choice of consecutive passages must be carefully made in order to cater for those making real progress and those still struggling. We must remember that a successful outreach group will be continually drawing in new people.

It has been shown that the average person can comfortably cope with no more than six weekly studies on the same subject or part of the Bible. A group which attempts to fight its way chapter by chapter through, say, Leviticus will not be long in existence! Many people prefer to stay with a series of studies for no more than four weeks. After that the interest will begin to wane.

In spite of the fact that a minority of the group might prefer to do consecutive studies all the time, we have found that the majority of the group prefers to have a mixed diet which still includes topics in between the series. And where a series lasts six weeks it has proved beneficial to have a break after three weeks for a topic, and to continue again after that.

A typical programme for a more mature group could be:

Sermon on the Mount—Matthew 6

1. Praying and giving secretly   —vv. 1-7 and 16-18
2. A model prayer   —vv. 8-15
3. God or Mammon   —vv. 19-24
4. God cares for us   —vv. 25-34
5. The Christian's route to Heaven—I Thess. 4
6. Why are we having these Bible Studies?

Men and Women of Faith in the O.T.

7. Ruth   —read ch. 1, vv. 1-5, 8 and 15-16.
             ch. 2, vv. 1, 2, 14.
             ch. 4, vv. 9-10, 16-22.
8. Daniel   —read ch. 3, v. 8 to ch. 4, v. 3.
9. David   —read I Sam. ch. 17, vv. 32-58.
10. Abraham —read Genesis 22, vv. 1-18.

Since one task of the leader is to help train other leaders he could at this juncture ask certain members to share his responsibilities by helping him plan the next programme of studies. Such a committee could meet every few weeks to pray and plan together. Recently we worked with a small committee consisting of Christians from quite a varied church and secular background. They came from F.I.E.C., Brethren and The Salvation Army and their occupations ranged from head gardener and salesman to accountant and business executive.

The Use of Missionaries and Speakers in the Programme

Before considering an invitation to a speaker it should be remembered that the basis of study is that of self-discovere from the Bible. As we shall see in Ch. 5, neither the leader nor a speaker should be the sole means of imparting knowledge and understanding to the group. I have attended many so-called Bible studies which have consisted simply of an address without any discussion or participation by the group. If a group is formed for the purpose of hearing ministry then by all means have ministry, but if it is to be a genuine study, then the majority of discussion should be by the members.

Bearing this in mind, we have found it advisable to invite a speaker only occasionally, say once every six weeks, and only then when the person concerned was someone who had something entirely relevant to say to the group. Sometimes we used a speaker to summarise a series of studies which we had been having and then to answer questions raised during the previous few weeks. On other occasions there were topics of particular interest such as "The work of the Gideons" in which a speaker would talk about the work of spreading God's Word. Again we have had speakers dealing with subjects like "prophecy and the return of Christ" and "The four different presentations of Christ in the Gospels" where the group would find it difficult to search for the great truths.

As a general rule a speaker was allowed 20-25 minutes for his opening remarks instead of the usual ten minutes, (see Ch. 5). This ensured discussion and question time for the rest of the hour. Sometimes a speaker felt led to continue for longer, but it was always made clear to them that twenty-five minutes was enough.

To bring members in touch with the overseas mission field we used to invite missionaries to come and talk about their work and to answer questions, thus stimulating an interest in God's work abroad. Even the seekers were affected by the dedication of these men and women who had given up so much to serve God. I well remember the general astonishment when a young man working in the Congo as a teacher told us his first task was to build the school! There are always many missionaries on furlough, and by contacting the home headquarters of various missions it is possible to find out when a missionary is in a particular area and available for meetings. Another useful source of such speakers is to contact local church leaders who will usually be in contact with possible speakers.

The Use of Tape Recordings and Films in the Programme

To add variety to the discussions and sometimes to fill in an awkward gap in the programme the leader may use tapes and films, the most suitable being those which allow sufficient time for discussion.

Tapes are available from many of the Christian organisations in this country and are usually loaned free of charge. Many of the well-known speakers who would not be able to accept an invitation to our home can then be heard by the group. In this way we have appreciated the ministry of such people as John Stott and Billy Graham. There are many Christians who would be very willing to make their tape recorders available to a group.

There is a variety of films and film strips available for home use, some at reduced rates. It is also possible to find teams which will provide projection equipment and run the film. It is, however, advisable for the leader to see the films himself before including them in the programme. Personal recommendations cannot always be relied upon, as we discovered one evening when a film highly commended turned out to be a complete non-starter.

Producing the Actual Programme Sheet

Today in every walk of life people expect the literature they receive to be of a high quality in its presentation. In offering a programme of Bible studies to our friends and neighbours we must be quite sure that it is of the best that we can produce. I have received a good deal of literature from churches and Christian organisations where both the typing and duplication leave much to be desired. It is really not honouring to the Lord to have work done in His service which is not up to the standard people expect. There is no need to produce a glossy printed leaflet for a home study but a clear duplicated sheet is much appreciated. It may be necessary to take the work to a professional, but we must be prepared to spend time as well as money if we are to glorify God in this work.

The duplicated sheet is invaluable to the members of the group. There are quite a number who will study the passages in advance. Others in the group cannot come every week and with a programme sheet they will be able to choose the studies most beneficial to them. And of course a home group grows by its members inviting others to the group and there is no better way of inviting them than by offering them literature which will attract their attention to what the studies are about.

Our experience has shown that one sheet should not cover more than ten weeks' studies, and after that the next should be issued. After ten weeks of being opened, folded, looked at, studied, crumpled, carted to and from meetings, stuck in a Bible, refolded, lent out, etc., the poor programme sheet has had about all it can take. We found that where a sheet covered more than ten weeks it usually ended up by getting lost. We watched with amusement as a friend absentmindedly made an aeroplane out of his programme sheet—and it was a new one, no less!

Although such sheets are duplicated, they can be made more personal by including the leader's address and telephone number and personal signature. The person's name to whom it is to be given should be written: "Dear Miss Smith".

These sheets should reach the members well in advance, preferably about ten days before the new studies begin. They may be handed out after a Bible Study, sent by post to those living further away, or delivered by hand where people live nearby. We found that personally delivering the sheets gave us the opportunity of talking to some who could not or did not attend so regularly. They were often encouraged by our interest in them.

A typical programme sheet might appear like this:

Tel: 321-2242

6 Burntash Road,
Moorside, Stockwell
July 21

Dear . . . ,

The following is a list of topics which have been suggested for the weekly Bible Study. As far as we can tell Wednesday night is still the best night for these studies. The topics will be discussed on the nights listed below from 8.00-9.00 p.m. Please tell your friends about this, or better still, bring them with you.

BIBLE STUDY PROGRAMME

Aug. 9.	The World in Need.
Aug. 16.	The Necessity of the Cross.
Aug. 23.	Should we Worry?
Aug. 30.	The Meaning of the Resurrection.
Sept. 6.	Why should we Pray?
Sept. 13.	Is the Bible Historically and Spiritually Inspired?
Sept. 20.	Miracles.
Sept. 27.	The Bible in my Life.
Oct. 4.	Where are the Prophets Today?
Oct. 11.	Lead us not into Temptation.
Oct. 18.	How does God Guide us?
Oct. 25.	What is the Church?
Nov. 1.	What is a Christian?

Yours sincerely,
DEREK AND NANCY COPLEY

Four

Personal Preparation

ALTHOUGH THE LEADER OF ANY DISCUSSION NEED NOT have endless degrees in theology, he should at least have a working knowledge of the Scriptures and of doctrine. In some cases an inexperienced leader may be able to count on other Christians in the group to help him out when difficulties arise but there is no guarantee that he can rely on them to do so especially if he is doing a pioneer work in a barren area. Indeed it might be a dangerous thing where there is no Christian present who can safely guide the group when basic doctrine is discussed, and many have been unwittingly led astray in this manner. Such a situation may be summed up as "the blind leading the blind!" It is for this reason that some ministers and church elders have discouraged the formation of house groups since they fear that such groups could fall into doctrinal error through no fault of their own.

In spite of the fact that a group leader spends much time studying the Scriptures and leading Bible Studies, he also needs to take in extra spiritual food for himself by reading, attending services in which the Word is expounded, and making a deeper study of the Bible for his own personal benefit. Some Christians get so involved in their specialised work for the Lord that they fail to be involved in activities designed to promote their general spiritual maturity. Such Christians become very one-sided in their outlook and occasionally feel that *their* work alone is being blessed by God!

One thing is certain, that when a leader begins a Bible Study, he should be thoroughly acquainted with the passage under consideration even if there are minor areas of his Biblical knowledge that are lacking. And provided the group discusses the chosen verses and other connected Scriptures or doctrines, the leader need not venture on ground with which he is unfamiliar. If he senses being out of his depth it would be wise carefully to draw that part of the discussion to a close and then study for himself the problem which has arisen. It is better to do this than possibly to allow false doctrine to creep into the discussion.

In this chapter I have attempted to outline the various steps in Bible study preparation. Much of the work involved is similar to the preparation of a sermon, except that in this case the leader expects the group to discover the truth for themselves, whereas in the sermon the preacher attempts to spoon-feed the truths to his hearers. I hardly need mention that, as with the preacher, his leadership will be effective only if God has personally spoken to him through the Scripture passage which he is helping others to understand. It also goes without saying that he should pray fervently that God will enlighten the members of the group concerning what they are reading.

Choosing the Passages for Topical Studies

In the last chapter I described the preparation of a programme of studies in which there could be both topical studies as well as those from consecutive passages. Where a topical study has been chosen one of the first tasks is to decide which passages in the Bible are relevant to the subject, and then to narrow it down to one, two, or three passages which will be used in the study.

Although I can thoroughly recommend preparing Bible studies from scratch, an inexperienced leader may take refuge in the many published books of Bible study notes. By acquiring a fairly wide selection of these, it is quite likely that most of the topics he will be preparing can be found in one of his books, even if they are not precisely the same as he needs. This book in particular contains a number of useful studies in the appendix to which the reader may refer. Some Christians feel that to use other people's material is a form of cheating, but I personally believe that we should use all the help that we can get so long as God's Word remains prominent in our thoughts and preparation. In any case, we do not need to use someone else's study word for word, we may simply use some of his ideas and passages of Scripture. I have *occasionally* made use of books of sermons by well-known preachers in which specific topics coincide with those chosen for our own studies, such as Dr. Martyn Lloyd-Jones' "Sermon on the Mount".

The real difficulty arises when a topic has been chosen and we cannot find any books, sermons, or other material from which to prepare a study. In Ch. 3 I mentioned that there are some topics on which the Bible remains silent, or at least which do not readily lend themselves to group discussions, and these are best avoided. But there are subjects such as peace with God, faith, guidance, heaven, worry, happiness, etc., which are quite suitable for discussion.

Let us take the subject of "worry" as an example. One of the most useful tools which every group leader should possess is a Bible concordance. These vary from the completely comprehensive ones where every word in the Bible is listed, to those which mention just the major words together with the reference. It is very unlikely that you will find the word "worry" in any concordance, but there will be other words connected with it for which there will be Bible references. Such words as troubled, care, thought, confidence, peace, mind, tomorrow, etc., come to mind and will provide several suitable passages for study. It is a good thing at this point to list the references on paper and read each one carefully, perhaps consulting a commentary where a verse seems obscure or irrelevant.

During the Bible Study itself it is best to limit the reading to three passages of Scripture at most; people become confused by too much material to study. This means that the number of references discovered in the concordance must be narrowed down to those which cover the topic adequately but without too much overlap. If you refer to to the Bible Study in the appendix entitled "Should we worry?" you will notice that each of the three passages contains something different on the subject. The verses in Philippians 4 state the principle that we are to pray and not to worry, those in Matthew 6 are the words of the Lord who shows how illogical worry is, and in Mark 4 we have an example of what worry really is, a failure to believe that God is in control of every situation. All the other verses I found contained the principles or examples found in these three passages.

It is often helpful to seek advice from more experienced Christians who have a greater familiarity with their Bibles than we have, and who can suggest suitable passages for study. I often used to spend an evening with a good Christian friend of mine and between us we not only planned a helpful Bible Study but had a good time of fellowship together. There may be another study group not too far away which has overcome many of its teething problems and has plenty of ideas to pass on. It is quite likely the group will have studied many of the topics in your own programme of studies and can give the pros and cons of the various passages they used. We ourselves have helped several groups in this way.

Choosing the Passages for Systematic Studies

One thing that should be emphasised here is that the average group cannot adequately cope with consecutive studies for more than about six weeks on any one book of the Bible. This is stressed in Ch. 3, which is concerned with planning Bible studies. There are not many books which can be covered in so short a time except perhaps the Minor Prophets or the shorter New Testament Epistles. Yet the group must be balanced in its spiritual diet and cannot ignore basic books like Genesis or any of the Gospels. Rather than plod through the longer books for many months, the home study group should concentrate on studies limited to only part of those books and then come back to the other parts at a later date. For example, in Genesis a series of studies in the life of Abraham could be followed at a later date by a series on Joseph. In Exodus, studies about the Passover could lead to a series involving the events taking place as the Children of Israel wandered in the desert.

In the New Testament, three sets of studies could be taken from the Sermon on the Mount in Matthew 5, 6 and 7, each lasting say four weeks. One might also consider studying four consecutively-recorded miracles or parables of the Lord. And of course, the account of the trial and crucifixion of the Lord is something which every group should study. The shorter epistles like Galatians, Ephesians, I Thessalonians, etc., are also suitable for study in this way.

One of the mistakes we made during our earlier studies was to try to cover too much ground in one evening. For example, we tried to study the life of Joseph in a single evening, also the famous prayer of the Lord in John 17. Each would really have been more profitable split up into several studies. Even studying one chapter a week of, say, Philippians can be rather rushed and much of the detail has to be left out of the discussion. But I still think that it is better to have four separate series of studies on an epistle than sixteen consecutive ones, if one chapter a week proves too much. In any case it is not always a bad thing if we do omit discussion of some details in a passage. The whole point of a home discussion group is to allow the Word of God to speak to each member rather than the group attempting a critical analysis of every verse. No doubt those who wish may do so privately with the help of a commentary. In fact, if the group Bible study method is effective, then individual members will begin their own personal study of the Bible, having been taught in the group to search the Scriptures and to apply them to daily life.

Anticipating the Study

In Ch. 5 there is a full description of the strategy of leading a Bible Study, together with thoughts and comments about various difficulties which arise. The basic purpose of a discussion group is that the group discovers the truths directly from the Bible and then each member relates these to this own life. If he is a Christian then he should be drawn closer to Christ by applying the Word to his life, if he is not yet committed to Christ then the application is obvious, the Bible will tell him he needs a Saviour and that he should put all his trust in Christ.

It therefore follows that the leader of a discussion group should anticipate that the majority of the time will be spent in purposeful discussion and that only a minority of the time should be allotted to him for his opening remarks. The basic pattern which should emerge is that of an opening prayer, a Scripture reading, a short introduction by the leader of, say, ten minutes, the time for discussion under guidance by the leader, and finally a closing prayer.

At this stage in his preparation the leader will need to work out what he will say as an introduction to the discussion, and to think about what kind of questions would be most suitable to bring out the Bible truths. He may wish to introduce each question separately during the discussion time or may simply suggest the questions as part of his introductory remarks and then allow members of the group to discuss them in their own time without too much regimentation. Much of the success or otherwise of the Bible Study will depend on his preparation before the meeting takes place.

Preparing the Introduction to the Study

One of the most important things that a group leader should remember is that his remarks are not to be an address but should stimulate the other members of the group to search the Scriptures and then obey what God says through the Bible. This is one reason why we decided to limit such remarks to ten minutes, which had the added advantage of leaving a full forty-five minutes for open discussion. Even so the sort of things said here in the ten minutes are quite different from what one would say in a ten-minute sermon. In the latter case it is often necessary to include only the more important truths in order to impart as much information to the hearer as possible. It is a mistake to try to present to a Bible study group too many conclusions and explanations because there will be little left for the group members to discover for themselves. Not only can this be a spiritual hindrance but it is also educationally bad to always spoonfeed those who are learning. Indeed the modern concept of programmed learning is based on the principle that the learner should continually build up his knowledge only upon facts that he has already understood. Such a concept does not favour the presentation of new, unrelated facts to the learner.

You may feel that the group may fail to find some of the deepest truths in the Bible if they study on the self-discovery basis. It is true that this will inevitably happen at first, but there is nothing to hinder the members repeating a Bible study at a later date when they are better equipped to dig out the hidden truths. Is this not exactly the way the Lord taught His own disciples? For example, His parables progressively contained deeper truths, and the understanding of one parable rested upon having grasped the meaning of the previous one.

The leader's remarks should give the group members enough information to help them to begin to use their Bibles effectively. For example, there may be one or two difficult words which need explaining, or an ambiguous verse which might cause confusion. He may need to direct the group to another translation which helps in the understanding of a particular passage. There is often background information which will aid the discussion, such as the authorship of an epistle or the historical period and social conditions prevalent when the verses were written or when the action took place. Most important of all he must stimulate the members to see what relevance a passage or verse has to their personal lives and circumstances. Without the application of the truth, the discussion is only of academic interest and the voice of God is stifled.

Detailed Preparation of a Study on Matthew 6: 19-34

In Ch. 3 we have explained how to plan a balanced programme of Bible Studies. Let us now suppose that there is to be a discussion of the Sermon on the Mount and the above-mentioned verses have been allocated to a particular week. Alternatively, the subject of money is under discussion as a "topical" study and the leader has decided that this passage would be helpful. The students of Moorlands Bible College recently prepared a Bible Study as part of their examinations, and I shall draw both good and bad examples from their efforts.

Before doing any detailed work on the passage, the leader should make a mental note of what he is trying to get out of it. His aims are basically the same as those of the preacher who is preparing a sermon, except that his desire is for the group to discover the truths for themselves. He should discover for himself three things from the passage:

1. What the passage says.
2. What the passage means.
3. How the passage applies.

Both his introduction and the discussion should be designed to fulfil these basic aims, especially No. 3. It is important that the Word of God speaks to the leader in a very real way before he can ever hope to encourage the group members to apply it to their own lives. However, the group should not place so much emphasis on the application that the first two aims are ignored, since this would lead to a search for Bible verses which fit in with the views of the group rather than vice versa.

1. *What the Passage Says*

To those of us who are familiar with the Bible this phase of preparation may appear to be trivial. But we must remember that if our group successfully draws in people who are untaught in the Scriptures, then we must help to guide them concerning the actual facts of the narrative. For example, the word "mammom" in Matt. 6: 24 is not readily understood, nor is the word "cubit" in 6: 27. The leader should find alternative words which convey the same meaning and include these in his introduction. There may also be certain verses where the language of the King James Version (K.J.V.) makes the meaning obscure. It would be a great help to the group to hear these verses in another translation, say, Phillips, Today's English Version (T.E.V.) or Revised Standard Version (R.S.V.)

2. *What the Passage Means*

Here the leader must be quite sure that he fully understand the passage himself. He should be familiar with the background to the verses as well as the context in which they occur. Since there are good commentaries on every book in the Bible there is no reason why he should not use the appropriate ones. Commentaries written on individual books of the Bible are very helpful, although one-volume works on the entire Bible are sometimes more suitable as they contain less detail for the leader to sift through.

The background to any Bible book is very important. Matthew's Gospel was written in order to convince Jews that Jesus was the Messiah, though of course it also speaks to the Gentiles. The context of the Sermon on the Mount should also be noted. It was addressed to his disciples (5: 1) who were living in the midst of a materialistic, religiously proud nation who cared more for the minute details of their view of the Law than for the spiritual meaning of it.

Before being concerned with the detail of each verse it is best to take a bird's-eye view of the whole passage. In this case it is a question of having the right attitude to material possessions and of seeing these things in their correct perspective. Although the group should search for the truth themselves, it may be helpful to explain the meaning of certain difficult verses such as 6: 22 where it talks about the light of the body being the eye, and 6: 23 where an evil eye is referred to. It is essential that the leader knows the meaning of the other verses, too, even if he says nothing about them in his introduction. Only by doing this can he help guide the discussion in such a way as to avoid totally wrong conclusions by the group.

3. *How the Passage Applies*

As I have already mentioned, the whole point of a Bible Study is that the Word bears fruit in the lives of its readers. It must be shown in the introduction that there is an application of the verses to the lives of people living today, particularly those present in the group. We all have material possessions and yet treasures in heaven (6:20) are more important. In acquiring these we must have singleness of purpose (6: 22, 23) since we cannot be a slave to both God and money (6: 24). For those who tend to worry about money these verses are full of encouragement to trust in a God who cares and will supply every need (6: 25-34). In particular, the key to joy and peace concerning these things is 6:33 where there is a definite promise that if we put God's interest first, He will take care of our material needs.

It is necessary to spend a good deal of time in prayer and meditation in preparing this part of the introduction because each member must be helped to make a personal application of the Bible truths. It is a very thrilling experience to listen to members' remarks as they discover for themselves that there is no need to worry about money so long as they put God first. It is not sufficient even for the group to come to a theoretical conclusion concerning other people, what has been learnt has to be put into action by them. It is no good coming to the conclusion that there are far too many people around seeking earthly wealth if each member does not examine his own heart to see if he is guilty of the same thing. And of course the group should see the urgency of carrying out what they have discovered rather than putting it off until a future date.

There is no easy way of explaining how the leader is to achieve these aims with his group, since to some extent it will very much depend on the group itself. But he must avoid the two extremes of saying too much and not saying enough, which results in the group missing the whole point of the study. If he has done his homework properly, the leader will know what conclusions he expects and hopes for from the discussion and by a few well-chosen remarks can help guide the conversation in the right direction.

Some groups prefer to have their thoughts stimulated by set questions for discussion; others are happier having the freedom to discuss points raised by the leader in his introduction. We used the latter method. In this case the leader does need to ensure that the group is disciplined enough to cover all the major issues from the passage. For those who use this way of studying, the set questions at the end of this book could be incorporated in the introduction and be suggested for discussion rather than be stated formally.

Preparing Questions for Discussion

The questions should be designed to bring out the three basic aims of the study as outlined earlier in this chapter. Questions designed to help the group understand what the passage says are not easy to prepare and often cause a one-sentence answer to be made, and so lead to no further discussion.

e.g. Where are we to lay up treasures?

Answer: In heaven.

Many Bible studies for young people use such questions as these in order to get members to refer to their Bibles, though we have not found these of very much help in adult work.

Questions involving "what the passage says" and "how the passage applies" are much more fruitful. The former bring out the doctrines of Christianity and the latter bring out the relevance of them to the twentieth-century Christian.

Here are some of the questions prepared by my students:-

Does this passage imply that a Christian must be poor?

How can we be sure our daily needs will be supplied?

What should we do with the money and possessions we've got?

Should we take a "couldn't care less" attitude to life?

What is the solution to eliminating anxiety?

How can we lay up treasures in heaven?

Should Christians take out life insurance?

Sometimes it is especially helpful to prepare questions which run in a definite sequence, each building on the foundation of an earlier one. In this particular passage there is a natural sequence of thoughts and the questions could direct the group to successive verses finishing with the conclusions in verses 33 and 34.

Other passages may have several themes or thoughts and before deciding on specific questions the leader should divide up the verses into a smaller number of sections, and prepare questions to bring out the main truth from each of these sections. It would help the group if he outlined these divisions in his introduction so that they could easily locate the section relevant to the question. Most commentaries divide their passages of Scripture into headings and sub-headings, and are useful for getting the maximum benefit from each chapter studied.

Providing Notes for Members

If the group is discussing set questions, it is useful to give a copy of the questions to each person present so that they can refresh their minds concerning the particular question being discussed. Many people appreciate receiving a copy of the leader's ten-minute introduction. A few brief notes will usually suffice. The summary should state the background and context of the passage, and difficult words or phrases should be explained. He should also include sufficient material to be of value to any member who keeps it for future use.

Bible Study Titles

Since many of you will have bought this book on impulse rather than basing your decision on reviews and articles about it, you will realise the value of a good title and presentation. Many who come to a Bible Study for the first time do so because they have seen an interesting-looking title for the subject under discussion.

In the previous chapter I mentioned the importance of finding non-theological titles since they would appear either dull or incomprehensible to the average member of the public. At the same time they should describe the real subject under discussion and not mislead people.

Some good titles prepared by my students were:-

Your God, Your Money and You.
Is Wealth the Answer?
What God has to say about Money.

First things First.
A Right Sense of Values.
So You want to be Rich!
God and Mammon.
True riches.

Other titles I received were either slightly unimaginative or did not point the reader to the subject. They were:-

Sit down and count the cost.
Practical Christianity.
Money and health.
How to get the best of both worlds.

Much of what has been written about preparing a Bible study may seem arduous and even unnecessary, but the whole point of the exercise is to make the Bible study for each member as easy as possible so that he can appropriate personal benefit from the discussion. A study *can* be prepared quickly and with little thought but I doubt if the group will derive as much profit from it as from one where every detail has been carefully and prayerfully considered by the leader. His task is to use every means possible to enable the group members to read their Bibles and to understand and apply what they read. When he has really done his own homework, then, and not until then, can he count upon God to do what he cannot do.

Five

Leading the Meeting

FIRST IMPRESSIONS ARE OFTEN LASTING IMPRESSIONS. IT IS our duty to be quite sure that our guests are aware that everything possible has been done to ensure their comfort and general sense of wellbeing. Our task is a public relations exercise, just as is the average kitchenware or lingerie party held in the home. The main difference is that we are offering something of eternal value, they are selling temporal goods. One thing which is noticeable about professionally sponsored home-selling parties is the high standard of preparation before the meeting. Christians often feel that it is unspiritual to do too much preparation and that prayer works wonders. Well, I agree that prayer is essential, but so is good, old-fashioned, hard work and thoughtfulness. Many of our churches could do with this ancient commodity—comfort. Although this is another subject, I can thoroughly recommend H. L. Ellison's *The Household Church*, in which he firmly dispels the idea that subjecting the public to discomfort is a spiritual exercise!

Our visitors should find our home as we would hope to find theirs—clean and fresh. Many of our homes would benefit from a breath of fresh air occasionally to blow away those nostalgic odours so frequently found in museums. I'm sure we all enjoy the appetising smell of frying onions or chips as we contemplate eating them but an hour after the meal it is a very different story! There are two solutions to this problem of cooking smells—apart from starving or

51

eating sandwiches before a study! One is to cook a meal which doesn't leave an offensive odour, the other is to use one of science's inventions—the aerosol spray.

For some obscure reason there are still Christians who regard personal hygiene as a worldly pursuit, while deodorants, mouth drops, perfumes and aftershaves are positive evils to be shunned. Surely those who are involved in the King's business should be quite sure that they are "nice to be near" by taking a few simple precautions. Remember next time you enter a crowded bus on a hot day and are met by a wall of B.O. that you too may be an unpleasant contributor at your home Bible study! And remember too that no one likes bad breath, so we should take care to avoid any foods which taint our breath, or suck a Polo before the meeting starts (as Dan Piatt used to advise counsellors working in Billy Graham crusades).

The following paragraph may give the readers the impression that what they need is a complete redecoration and refurnishing of their houses and that only the well-to-do should attempt Bible Studies. Far from it, the most humble home can be charmingly adapted for the purposes of our Lord's work. What is needed mostly is thought and consideration for others.

Preparing the Room for the Meeting

It is not always easy to provide perfect seating arrangements since most of us do not own enough chairs or a room which is large enough. But by arranging the chairs in something resembling a circle and removing obstacles like small tables, aspidistras and T.V's it is possible to seat quite a number in a small room. Naturally all this takes time and effort. Our own activities during the hour preceding the meeting resembled a cross between moving house and Piccadilly Circus during rush hour. Our neighbours were often very kind and loaned us anything from chairs to crockery if the need arose. While soft, diffused lighting is very nice for some purposes, it is not always adequate for seeing Bibles, especially when some people insist on using editions with minute print. Temperature, too, has a profound effect on the group. At first we varied between freezing and wilting since our coal fire simply would not obey the command to become instantly cooler or hotter. For those with central heating the problem is not so bad, but any other form of heating presents problems. Being of a scientific inclination, I eventually discovered just how big the fire should be, allowing for the wattage of, say, twenty people engaged in hot study. Older guests prefer to be near a source of heat, although even then they may like to keep their coats and gloves on. It follows of course that the leader should have a chair in a position where everyone can see him.

Having Modern Translations Available

Some visitors will inevitably come without Bibles and it is better to supply them with a copy at the meeting then to ask them to share. In addition, Bible studies are often much better if members have a variety of translations, especially the more up-to-date ones like Phillips and Today's English Version. Many people found that whereas the K.J.V. was sometimes unintelligible, the modern rendering was a great help. There are always those in each group who sincereld believe that the K.J.V. is the only inspired version any refuse to use any other. We had one dear Christian lady in our group who loved her K.J.V. so much that we laughingly tried for three years to persuade her to try another version, but to no avail.

I found it a good practice to go round the group at the start of a study and distribute various translations to those who wanted them.

Refreshments

It is usual to provide some kind of refreshments either

before, during or after the study. For an adult Bible study there is less distraction when they are served immediately after the study is over. This emphasizes the importance of starting and finishing promptly. To speed things up, the water for tea-making should be boiled before the meeting so that it takes little time to boil when making the tea, since it is already hot. A selection of biscuits should be ready in advance, placed on one or more suitable plates. Those large tins of assorted biscuits are suitable and cheaper than buying smaller packets. Many hosts fall into the trap of trying to provide a more elaborate spread than this, which eventually evolves into almost a full-scale meal. Apart from the obvious cost of such a practice, there is another disadvantage. Some groups move from house to house and it is quite likely that some are unable to afford more than a biscuit and a cup of tea. We ourselves observed a group in which the fare grew more lavish each week until it reached the scale when a poorer member was too embarrassed to be hostess and it seriously damaged her Christian life.

The Timing of the Meeting

There is a saying that you should start as you mean to go on. Having invited people to a study at 8 p.m. finishing at 9 p.m. we fully intended to keep to our promise by starting and finishing promptly. By actually starting our first meeting just before 8 o'clock, it ensured that guests would arrive early in the future. And they did too. Only after one major catastrophe did we ever start late during the period of three years. This occurred because we had decided to buy a new three-piece suite and offered the old one for sale at five pounds. The proud purchaser of our old suite decided without telling us, to collect it on a certain Wednesday night at exactly 8 p.m., and there he was outside the door with a hand cart. Amid much laughter, the group gallantly helped to remove our furniture into the street, and after borrowing extra chairs we duly began the study ten minutes late!

It is surprising how many people told us of their appreciation of the strict timing of our studies. Today many people have so little time to spare that they cannot afford to waste any. One member of the group was a lady whose husband was in rather poor health and was not happy about her arriving home much after 9 p.m. This was one instance in which prompt finishing of the study and my wife's efficient tea-making made it possible for this member to be out of the house before 9.15. Please do not think that every type of Bible Study must be kept in order by such strict timing—there are many where this would be a real mistake. For example, Young Wives' groups may prefer to be very flexible about starting and finishing; I am told that it suits the temperament of the female sex. Young people often like much longer studies especially if they happen to be students. Several years ago the Christian Union at Manchester University decided to run a special series of basic Bible studies for young Christians and invited me to be the leader. The discussions were so lively that we frequently continued into the early hours of the morning when I had obviously missed the last bus and had to *walk* the five miles home.

Perhaps the most obvious advantage in finishing on time was a psychological one. By 8.55 the group had really loosened up and the discussion was lively and stimulating, and some would suggest that to stop it then would be a major disaster. By calling a halt at this stage when things were really interesting, each member of the group was eager to come back again next time. Occasionally when the discussion seemed to be flagging and we had not yet reached the appointed hour it was best to suggest that we finish and have our cup of tea early. It isn't always easy to ensure that each discussion lasts exactly an hour and a hesitant, artificially-enlivened last few minutes is not worth using since it leaves the people in a state of anticlimax.

Since I have said nothing about the study itself, it might

seem inappropriate to talk about what happens when its over, but nevertheless some of the most important work is done later in the evening. Many people who come to home study groups do so because they have special needs or problems. Although we were very firm about our timing of the formal study period we always made it clear that people were under no obligation to go home once things had finished. Some of the most valuable counselling was done later in the evening. We found that most people would not publicly discuss their deepest problems but preferred to talk privately after the others had gone home. We even had members who left our house apparently on their way home, only to reappear when they thought everyone else had gone. After a while we used to expect one or two to sneak back each week for a chat. We were sometimes amused when people returned to our house only to discover that others had the same idea! Rather than take up valuable space here the whole question of pastoral care will be discussed in Ch. 6.

The Early Arrivers

When the guests do arrive, they ought to find everything ready both for the meeting itself and for the cup of tea afterwards. This of course includes setting out sufficient cups, saucers and spoons in another room or in the kitchen. At first it seemed to take hours to prepare for the studies, but after a few weeks we soon established a routine. There are some guests who like to arrive early for a chat some even used to come to help an hour before they were due. One can be taken quite unawares when this happens the first time, with the hostess getting changed upstairs, and the gallant host staggering beneath a load of unwanted furniture. If things were not ready as early as this, our main defence was to usher the visitor to an undisturbed corner of the room and leave a pile of National Geographic magazines handy or even a selection of Christian literature.

Greeting the Guests

It would be courteous to enquire a day or two or even the week before how certain guests are to travel to the study. Some, maybe those living quite a distance away, or those either elderly or in poor health, may need transport. We ourselves did not have a car and relied on others to provide lifts. There may be some living quite near who prefer to be accompanied, especially during the dark nights.

Coats should be removed from guests as they arrive, unless they indicate otherwise. Remembering names is guaranteed to make them feel welcome, also information about how to find the bathroom and toilet.

The Start—Getting to Know Each Other

So our members have arrived and are awaiting some action from the leaders. Most people feel shy and perhaps rather silly sitting in a circle with comparative strangers surrounding them. Although we ourselves knew everyone's name they certainly didn't know each other's. It's not easy or convenient to introduce each person to everyone individually; indeed, mathematically that would be a very large number of introductions—I suppose in a group of thirty it could amount to some four hundred! Although it seemed rather childish to go round the circle saying their names, addresses and church connexions (if any), what else could we do? We hesitated to put a label on people as they came in, as one might do at a formal conference. So we asked each one to say a word about himself or herself. We did this for a few weeks until they all knew each other and the atmosphere was usually so cordial that no one felt embarrassed about forgetting a name after that. Of course, we always introduced new members, to make them feel welcome, and especially during the first year of studies was this necessary, as during this time there were over one-hundred-and-fifty different visitors.

The Opening Remarks

In spite of the extensive advertising telling us to be different from other people and to be independently-minded, people still enjoy a certain amount of routine in their lives. Books on psychology tell us that young children become emotionally disturbed when their routine is broken. So do I when my meal is late! I suppose this is why most churches have some kind of liturgy or order of service. Some Christians, of course, don't like such routine as it is considered unspiritual, but that's another matter! For several weeks I used to outline to the group at the beginning of each study what was going to happen. I would explain (a) the purposes of the study, to give us all a better understanding of the Bible and to deepen our personal faith in Jesus Christ, and then (b) outline the procedure which we adopted quite early on, that is, a ten-minute introduction followed by a discussion. (c) After a short prayer (d) I would ask for a volunteer to read the verses to be studied. (e) I would then spend a maximum of ten minutes introducing the study, leaving a full forty-five minutes for discussion.

The Opening Prayer

Following these opening remarks we usually had a short prayer. I usually took this responsibility though later the more vocal and experienced men in the group readily participated in this way. However, I always asked them privately in advance if they would like to pray. Sometimes they said no. My prayers were always brief and very specific, avoiding King James English or clichés not easily recognised by the untaught members. There are many who sincerely believe that it is irreverent to use normal everyday English when addressing God, though I cannot honestly say that God has failed to answer my prayers on the occasions when they have been in a modern tongue. I have noticed in the last few years how many Christian leaders are changing their public praying habits. The ancient and beautiful language of King James' day is gradually being reserved for the more formal occasions. There may be some readers who are themselves not used to praying in front of others in an extemporary manner. I can vividly remember my first attempt when for hours I had planned and memorised what to say and on the occasion itself everything got muddled up. May I suggest writing down a short prayer and then simply reading it? I think evangelicals such as ourselves have been somewhat brainwashed into thinking that this is not very spiritual. But we prepare sermons and Bible studies, so why not prayers too if we feel the need?

Reading the Scriptures

Our next item was usually the Scripture reading. In Ch. 4 you may have noticed that one can only use a maximum of three passages in a study on any given occasion, partly because of the shortness of people's memories, partly shortage of fingers to insert in the various pages. It was usually possible to find a volunteer to read the passages. To help the reader, the leader should carefully pronounce difficult names or words or simply suggest that if they get stuck to leave them out altogether. Have you ever tried reading aloud a passage containing unpronounceable names? I don't like the method of reading a verse at a time round the group, for at least two reasons. First, there is a lack of continuity, since each voice has a different sound and emphasis and speed of reading and since there will always be a variety of translations present which might cause confusion, especially those versions with no individually numbered verses. Second, it forces people to open their mouths publicly and there are many who simply shrivel up at the thought of it. I know that each person has already had to say their name, but that's different. Today many people have never read the Bible at all and to read in public what in their case could well be a difficult verse would prevent them from ever coming back again. We have had numerous testimonies from group members to the fact that they would not have continued coming if anyone had made them speak. It may be a rather negative quality of our group, but it was one which was much appreciated. We had one member who only spoke once in the discussion in three years yet his life was enriched and blessed because he was able just to sit and listen. I realise that this goes against the advice of most manuals on leadership, which stress the importance of getting everyone to take part.

My wife attended a study last summer in which the leader overcame the problem of an individual speaking alone in public by asking the group to read aloud all at the same time. If they had all been using the same translation this would have been a good idea. But they weren't. It was quite a sound, vaguely reminiscent of a women's tea-party, or the people attempting to converse with each other after the judgement of Babel.

As time went on the reading was generally done more or less alternately by two ladies who liked to use the modern translations. Scripture reading may seem such a simple procedure that many groups fail to realise that the way it is done can either make the whole meeting relaxed or cause anxiety to inexperienced members. For example, the average person does not know where the books of the Bible are. Nor did I when I was first converted. So the leader should give some help to the group members by guiding them to the right place. We used a passage from Hebrews on one occasion and had failed to mention where it came. One poor soul was wading through the lesser Prophets since it sounded like an Old Testament book. For Old Testament books guidance can be given by repeating the names of the books in order up to the one desired, or if near the end of the Old Testament it is best to work backwards. The same applies to the New Testament. Up to II Thessalonians begin

at Matthew and end at the chosen passage, but from I
Timothy onwards going backwards from Revelation is
helpful.

Some people take ages finding their places, or end up in
John's gospel when it should be one of his Epistles and are
generally embarrassed about the whole thing. The biggest
obstacle in all Bible studies is the fact that you are asking
people who are unchurched and untaught to study something completely outside their own experience. At every
stage of the study we must ensure that people feel completely relaxed. A helping hand from someone sitting near
the confused person will quickly open the right page for
them. My wife has developed through much practice the
art of being stupid! She can readily fail to find the correct
passage on any occasion when another member is having
difficulties and thus make them not feel too badly about it. I
never thought that the Lord could bless such deliberate
stupidity! Many years ago when I was a teenager out to
tea I spilt a little salad cream on the tablecloth and felt
very embarrassed about it. My embarrassment soon
disappeared as my host deliberately knocked the cream jug
over and made a much worse mess. I didn't realise it at the
time but she was simply doing her best to make me feel
at home.

The Leader's Introduction

In Ch. 4 I described what is involved in preparing the
Bible Study. You will remember that I suggested an
introduction by the leader followed by the discussion.
There are two ways of leading the discussion. One is simply
to let the group discuss points raised in the introduction,
the other is a more regimented way, namely having specific
questions to be answered by the group. With an inexperienced group the latter can be a good way of drawing out
the members.

I have already mentioned in Ch. 4 the general contents of

the introduction and how to go about preparing suitable questions for discussion. Although many group leaders have been diligent in their work before a study begins they fall into the trap of turning the introduction into a sermon which not only covers too much material and gives the answers which the group should discuss for themselves, but also takes up too much time. The problem of drying up too soon, which afflicts the new leader, soon disappears and the opposite becomes the real problem. If the group senses that it has an expert in the midst, namely the leader or anyone else for that matter, it will stifle many members who feel inadequate. People are easily put off if they think someone is there who knows much more than they do. I feel personally that many groups fail to grow spiritually because they are not allowed to discover the great truths of Christianity for themselves, and make an application of them to their own lives. The more discussion by the group and the less direct spoon-feeding by the leader the greater I believe will be God's blessing. Of course this is not to suggest that Christians should never be spoon-fed; one of the great functions of the local church is to teach its members and to use its men of gift to impart the divine truths. It is a pity that more people do not sit under the ministry of these great servants of God. But we are discussing a home Bible study where self-discovery is the basic aim.

There is no divine inspiration in choosing a maximum of ten minutes for an introduction, but it has proved to be a useful choice. Our way of making sure that this was not exceeded, was by team work. My wife, being a good clock-watcher, used to wave a watch at me when the time had elapsed, and that was that. The group was very good-humoured and my rapid concluding remarks were accompanied by considerable mirth.

It really makes little difference to the technique of leadership whether there are set questions to discuss or whether the ideas raised in the introduction are talked about with gentle guidance as to the general direction of the discussion.

Getting the Discussion Going

The beginning of the discussion often sets the tone of the whole meeting, but it was also the most difficult part of it. Most people take a little while to thaw out and some feel able to participate only in the last ten minutes or so. Many young people's groups have one or two stooges who get the discussion going if no one else does. The others are then encouraged to say something. My wife was always ready to set the ball rolling and often did it by means of a very simple enquiry about something I had said in the discussion, though always directing the question to the group rather than to me. As in the case of finding the passage to read, she often feigned stupidity by raising a point which would obviously cause some to open their mouths. For example, in a study on forgiveness of sins the stooge could suggest that since Christ died for the sin of the world (John 1: 29) then everyone's sins are automatically forgiven. Such a remark immediately puts the discussion on a personal level and eventually by reference to whatever passage is under consideration, the group will discover that each must individually put his or her trust in Christ. Again, feigned ignorance not only helps to start a discussion but makes the members feel at home.

As you may have noticed, this is the second situation in which my wife used to feel it necessary to pretend to be ignorant. (The first was her apparent inability to locate the Scripture passage). Some readers with more tender consciences may wonder whether it is right to behave in this way! Paul in his first letter to the Corinthians explains how he reached people with the Gospel by being sensitive to their needs: "To the Jews I was a Jew that I might win the Jews. To those who were under the Law I put myself in the position of being under the Law (although in fact I stand free of it), that I might win those who are under the Law. To those who had no Law I myself became like a man without the Law (even though in fact I cannot be a lawless man, for I am bound by the Law of Christ), so that I might win the men who have no Law. To the weak I became a weak man, that I might win the weak. I have, in short, been all things to all men that by every possible means I might win some to God. I do all this for the sake of the Gospel; I want to play my part in it properly" (I Cor. 9: 20-23, Phillips). This passage convinces me that there is a Scriptural precedent for doing our utmost to make people feel at home during a study.

The most important task of the leader is to direct the group to the Bible by whatever means he is able. He should always bear in mind the mighty power of God's Word in influencing each of our lives. If he has prepared his introduction properly then the attention will have been centred on the passage in question. Although many members will have their own opinions about all kinds of things, it must be tactfully pointed out that any conclusions should be found in the passage under study or somewhere else in the Bible. Thus the group will gradually become Bible-centred and consequently Christ-centred. I have attended several Bible studies in which the Bible has neither been opened by the leader nor by the group, and I personally received very little blessing .Whenever someone quotes a verse to support a remark, especially if it lies outside the suggested verses, each member should be asked to find the verse and look at it for a moment. After a year of these studies one middle-aged man said that his knowledge of the Bible had increased in leaps and bounds since attending the discussion, simply because of the frequent quotation of verses. Some leaders may feel that the stifling of protracted discussions on politics or euthanasia would frighten people away, but we never felt this to be the case. People today often do hunger and thirst after Bible-based truth because deep down they realise that it contains the Word of Life rather than mere human opinion.

Sometimes I think we don't quite realise that the Word is truly living and able to give genuine spiritual enlightenment. Yet we have the testimony of members who have come to know Christ through the studies and Christians who have discovered a new joy and fulness in their lives because the Word drew them closer to Him. It is not easy to describe the transformations we have seen with our own eyes, but one member described it as resembling scales falling from his eyes. I don't think at the time he realised just how Biblical his remark was!

The Question-and-Answer Technique

If the group is using set questions prepared by the leader then his task will be to try to ensure that the group covers all the ground he feels necessary to a full understanding of the topic or passage. The technique then would be to state the question, gently guide the discussion and finally summarise what the group has discovered. Each question would then be answered and the members would have heard a concise statement of what they had found.

The Free Discussion Technique

We have tried the question-and-answer method of study a number of times but found that it was not so effective as that of letting the group discuss freely points raised by what was said during the ten-minute introduction. This is probably because it is a more natural way of talking together. When people visit us at home and they tell us about something in which we are interested, the conversation then flows quite naturally without their needing to state questions for discussion. It is not every group that can participate in this way, in spite of a good introduction to the subject by the leader. Of course, it follows that the leader by a few well-chosen remarks will be able to guide the group along certain lines in order to discover the important truths, even if they are not discussing set questions. It often happened that with only ten minutes left of discussion time, a major point raised by the leader at the beginning had not been discussed at all. For example, in a study on worldly wealth from the Sermon on the Mount using Matthew 6: 19-34 there may have been much discussion on the use and abuse of money, especially relevant to those members who are fairly well off. But for the others who might worry about money it would be helpful to direct the discussion towards the latter part of the chapter where the Lord made it clear that our Heavenly Father will look after all our needs. The leader can then say "Well now, we have only about ten minutes left, let us have a look at verses 25 to 34."

Difficulties

Bible study groups seem to be a mixture of complete opposites. There will be shy members who will not participate but alongside them will be some who talk too much and who need restraining. Together with those who know absolutely nothing of the Scriptures, who are liable to make incorrect remarks, we have mature Christians whose abundance of knowledge is off-putting to other members. Perhaps the biggest problem with mature Christians is the tendency to use what one might call jargon. This varies between King James English and evangelicalisms. Apart from the fact that King James language is difficult to follow, it contains many theological expressions which are meaningless to most people.

The Shy Ones

But how are shy people to be encouraged to participate? Perhaps the real question is whether it is possible for them to receive a blessing without saying anything in a group discussion. I believe the answer is a definite "Yes!" Some leaders feel they have partially failed if each one does not

open his or her mouth. To return to what we said earlier
about trying to make people feel at home and having a
natural atmosphere, in any social gathering in a home
there are those who remain silent, and they enjoy themselves
just the same. So why do we feel that each person must
talk in our discussion of the Bible? The Lord can surely
bless a person who simply prefers to listen. As we said
earlier, we had a man in our group who spoke only once in
three years, but his spiritual life, and even his own married
happiness deepened considerably as time went on.

One of the real fears of a shy person is that when they do
say something it will sound silly or irrelevant. Such an
individual will be encouraged beyond measure if when
they make a remark the leader emphasises what a good
remark it has been and how helpful to the group. I think that
something positive to say can always be found when a shy
person has plucked up courage to say something. This is
far better than snubbing them or making them feel that
their remark was not valued. We often found that their
remarks were made in a rather quiet voice which was
not always audible. It is the task of the leader to try to
sense that they are trying to say something and to make
sure they get the opportunity. We must remember that
many people in a group situation are rather like very young
children, full of eagerness to say the right thing but afraid
of the reactions of others. We must be gentle and kind
until they can find their own feet.

The Over-talkative Ones

As far as the group is concerned the over-talkative
member is much more of a problem. They may be either
well-taught, committed Christians or seekers who are
really basing their remarks on opinion rather than the Bible.
By gently showing the group that their comments should
spring from what the Bible says, the whole discussion will
be relevant and protracted comments based merely on

opinions are cut down. But how do you avoid too much lengthy participation by the Christians?

It is obviously impolite to ask anyone publicly to be silent. Hopefully the majority of the Christians will be aware that they could put others off by appearing too knowledgeable. During the discussion itself the leader may suggest that those who have already taken part should not speak for say ten minutes so that there are openings for others in the group. He may also tactfully ask that those who know the answers should wait until others have had a chance to discover the answer for themselves from the Scriptures. If these tactics fail, as sometimes they do, the last resort is to talk privately to the member concerned, and briefly mention the problem. This is not easy and occasionally not pleasant but the group must come first, and if the question is raised courteously and graciously there will be no hurt feelings. Most well-taught Christians I am sure do not realise that the whole aim is for the others to search for the truths. At your initial planning meeting this principle of self-discovery of the truth must be hammered home to the more knowledgeable Christians present.

It is particularly difficult when certain individuals attend Bible studies with a denominational axe to grind or a rather narrow viewpoint which they feel they should put over to the group. In spite of their sincerity the presence of such people can be devastating to the other members. As with the over-talkative ones, the leader should seek to encourage them to participate in the discussion in a general way without continually emphasing their own particular interest. It may seem harsh and unchristian, but I seriously suggest that if the problem cannot be solved politely the offender should be graciously asked to stay away from the studies until he or she is prepared to cooperate.

The Use of Evangelical Jargon

Those of us who have been Christians for some time have

usually absorbed a good deal of evangelical jargon. The real problem is that we don't realise it! But visitors to our discussion group certainly notice that Christians speak a language all of their own. We tend to pray in seventeenth century English, making obscure references to "that one of old" or "the Jewish economy" all of which is most confusing to the unlearned visitor. Not only that but we regularly use words in our comments which are either jargon or else Scriptural terms which are of course correct in themselves but not meaningful to many of the group. Typical teaching can also be a snare to the unwary!

From the very first meeting I made it clear that that if anyone used a term not readily understandable they should explain it to the group. But we use these terms so freely in our Churches that we often don't realise which words would confuse people. As group leader I felt it my duty to ask people to explain anything difficult, though I usually did it in a lighthearted way by saying "that's a theological-sounding word, would you tell us what it means?" Even the reference to the word Calvary, so dear to us Christians, does not always convey anything clear to someone who knows nothing of the Gospels. Expressions like "Oh, that's a Romans seven experience" may be very plainly understood by a few but how much better it is to turn to the chapter in question and explain it. Although we need not indulge in what is called "programmed learning" in a formal way, the discussion by the group should be on the basis of each new truth or idea being founded upon something already known and understood. Commercial enterprises take great pains to see that their product is described to the general public in terms they can understand. Our product, Christianity, should be so presented to the group members. As a general rule whenever anyone makes a comment he should think to himself "would that make sense to a complete stranger?" And if a short prayer is said before and after the discussion then I suggest it be in plain English, although it is not always easy to be bilingual, having one language for Church use and another for the discussion group.

Tactfully Handling Wrong Remarks

It is not unusual for a person to get hold of the wrong end of the stick and make a totally inappropriate remark. But at least he is trying to understand the passage. One's first thought is either to bury one's head in one's hands in despair, or to tell the person he's wrong. Neither action is of the least value! The leader who doesn't mind verging on white lies may say a very hesitant "Yes?" but perhaps a better way is to ask the group if there are any other ideas on the subject. This avoids telling the unfortunate member that he's wrong and helps bring out the right answer. One habit that we Christians tend to have is that of offending unbelievers by putting them in the wrong all the time. Even in psychiatric counselling, the doctor must never admit that he is shocked by what he hears, and his task is not to tell his patient how wrong he is, but by careful discussion and listening, he allows the patient to discover for himself where he has gone wrong. It is true that there is such a thing as the offence of the Cross and that is perfectly Biblical and to be expected, but there should not be any offence given as a result of my lack of tactfulness and consideration. The gospel is one of grace and I believe should be presented graciously.

Differences of Opinion

Home discussion groups can often be the arena for lengthy discussions and arguments. While these are fascinating to listen to and invigorating to take part in, they do not really represent the most effective way of studying the Bible. For one thing the group may miss the chance to study all the other aspects of the passage for lack of time, and for another such a discussion excludes the rest of the group while it is going on. The leader should be able to curtail the talking by stopping the participants tactfully and summing up both points of view, after which the group discussion should continue. If the long argument was about a Biblical subject suitable for a group study, then of course the leader could reserve a whole evening in the future for it. If the subject which arises is a so-called "red herring," totally irrelevant and perhaps engendering a bit of ill-feeling amongst some in the group, the leader's approach to the person must be especially tactful. He should find something positive to say about the subject and suggest that the group get back to a discussion of the Scriptures at hand. For example, someone grinding his axe for Methodism might cause ruffled feathers amongst the Baptists or Presbyterians in the group.

One of the results of the discussion being monopolised in this way is that the rest of the group feels left out and eventually other dialogues begin to take place between those who are bored or who wish to study the chosen passage. We have experienced these multiple discussions on several occasions and it has been necessary to call the meeting to order.

Awkward Silences

Many manuals on the techniques of leading Bible Studies emphasise the need to avoid silences during a discussion. But I think there is a difference between an embarrassing silence and one in which group members are genuinely searching the Scriptures before making any comments. In this case, the silence is profitable and may even give a chance to the shy members to make a few remarks. Naturally if the period of quietness goes on too long then the leader should say a few words to help start the discussion again, but I do not think that he needs to do this every time the talking stops.

The Leader's Role in The Discussion

Although a leader must at all times try to be merely a member of his group, he is often placed on a pedestal quite unwittingly when people begin to direct their questions to him rather than allowing the group as a whole to discuss things in an entirely natural way. If this happens, it is best to feign ignorance of the answer and throw the questions back to the rest of the group.

Perhaps the most important work of all for the leader is to avoid irrelevant discussion and to guide the conversation towards the application of Scripture to the life of each member. Unless the Word speaks individually to each person the discussion is only of academic interest. The few comments made by him during the study or the questions prepared beforehand can make the difference between a barren discussion and a genuine blessing. I have outlined in Ch. 4 the kind of remarks and questions most suitable for drawing group members into the discussion and causing them to become Bible-centred in their study and Christ-centred in their lives.

Six

Pastoral Care

IN MANY WAYS THE HOUSE GROUP HAS A RELATIONSHIP TO the local church similar to that which the local church has to the Universal Church, Christ's body. To a certain extent it is a church in miniature just as the local one is a small unit within the entire church. This means that the group and especially the leaders have certain pastoral responsibilities. To take the analogy too far, of course, would cause such a group to regard itself as a local church which it certainly isn't and never should be. If the group develops into a public testimony in an area devoid of evangelical witness that is fine, but if the group is run by members of a church in the area where that church is situated then the group should not attempt to replace that church. In this case the house group is simply one of the church's many different outreach efforts.

We often hear it said that the way to a man's heart is through his stomach. While this may be nonsense anatomically speaking, there is a good deal of truth in it. Many a young man's heart has been favourably disposed towards his true-love after tasting her excellent cooking. What I am getting at here is that humanly speaking many a person has been won for Christ by the general care and concern for their well-being by the Christian seeking their conversion. Too often we feel that having offered a gospel tract or invited someone to a gospel rally our duty to them and to the Lord has been fully discharged. Some of my students expressed surprise when I suggested that they should not only distribute tracts to the houses locally but should also talk to the people about their own interests, jobs, families, etc. While it is true that Christ came to save souls, He spent a great deal of time caring for their bodies too!

Much of life today has lost its personal touch and so many people long for real friendship and someone to whom they can turn. There are a large number of people whose relationship with Jesus Christ was preceded by a happy relationship with a Christian who took the trouble to be a real friend and not just a carrier of the gospel message. It is true that a Christian is "in" the world but not "of" the world, yet I do not believe that this precludes genuine friendships with unbelievers. Although Jesus hated sin, He always loved the sinner, just as the Christian is to hate what the Bible calls "the world" (I John 2: 15) but must not hate the people in it. I think that we have the tendency to interpret the principle of separation from evil as one of isolation from people and society. For many, this is the easy way out because it takes a lot of effort to be in contact with people yet avoiding compromise with evil.

But to return to the whole point of this chapter, the group which will be effective is the one which has found the balance between the two opposite extremes of compromise and isolation, between preaching only a social gospel and degenerating into a closely knit "holier than thou" Christian community. We must be very aware of the real physical needs of others yet at the same time not lose sight of the glorious Person of Christ whom we are seeking to present.

Let me say a few words about the cost of being of real value to other people in a pastoral sense. It will cost an enormous amount to the group and especially to the leader both in terms of money, time and energy. I do not think that a group leader can effectively do much else in his church except that which is expected of normal church members. In turn, if a church commends some of its members to an evangelistic ministry of this kind, then it should realise the immensity of the task and be faithful in prayer and encouragement. I would say that if the Christian leaders involved in this type of work are not prepared to put all they have got into it, then they should think twice before launching out.

The financial burden of the work will vary greatly from one situation to another. There will be some who will need to forego overtime work in order to give them time to visit. Provision of refreshments, though small in cost, can add up to a substantial sum over a period of time. We were very blest in this respect; the Christians in the group were extremely generous with money and gifts in kind. As part of our pastoral care, we used to have a Christmas party each year and provide a real spread of appetizing food, not to mention other social occasions provided for informal chatting. You soon discover that people with a spiritual hunger often have a financial need too, and this should be met. I suggest that this should be done anonymously since people feel uneasy about accepting money or gifts. Many groups need literature and Bibles, speakers should receive expenses, films have to be hired and a host of other things need to be paid for.

Perhaps one of the most costly of our possessions which we can offer to God is our time. While many Christians find it relatively easy to support God's work by helping financially, there are all too few who are able to give more than a few hours a week to the Lord. People are desperately looking for a sympathetic ear, the chance to unburden themselves to someone who is not in a hurry to get away. Group leaders especially are held in high esteem by members of their groups, and should be ready to talk to and counsel people at any time.

We recently talked to a Christian lady who had experienced many severe spiritual and physical difficulties and had sought help from her minister. In spite of being a very busy man he always gave the impression of having all the time in the world to talk to her. It was the self-sacrificing personal interest that really helped this lady, who knew that as long as she wanted to talk, he would be willing to listen. Perhaps we have all experienced seeking advice from a person who is continually looking at his watch and generally appearing agitated about the time.

Many group members appreciate being visited regularly in their homes and also receiving invitations to the leader's home. Ladies especially like to be visited by the man of the house! My wife used to visit people regularly but, with the elderly ladies especially, she always got the impression that they did not consider her visit to be a "proper" one, only a stop-gap measure until I could call personally and talk with them.

Many people find life rather humdrum and love to be invited out to tea or supper. We regularly had visitors in our home and although we really planned these for the benefit of our guests, we used to have some marvellous times together. Its not easy to get to know each other even in an informal house meeting but opening the home to individuals at other times is quite a useful way of building up their confidence in us and, of course, in the Lord.

Usually every group has one or two handymen in it who can offer their services to those less skilled in these matters. Often a simple thing like fitting an electric plug to an appliance or mending a fuse can be of tremendous benefit. In every area there are widows who have been used to their late husbands doing these little jobs and who are most grateful to group members who can help. We cannot tell just what will be the deciding factor in a person committing themselves to Christ, but it may only be a small act of love by a Christian. Sometimes illness or old age prevents neighbours from shopping or collecting their pensions, etc., and it only takes a little effort for a lady to offer her services by perhaps buying the few extra items needed.

Help should be offered tactfully because some do not like to accept what they call charity and often fear that they are causing inconvenience. Without forcing our offer upon them we should get over to them that it's really no trouble at all for us to assist them.

One of the highlights of our work was the annual Christmas party. It was really planned as a way of saying "thank you" to the group for all the joy they had brought to us and to show that we believed in good honest fun. And what fun we had too, mainly because we didn't try to Christianise the party by subjecting people to long messages and Bible quizzes. We simply spent the first ninety minutes playing good wholesome party-games and generally letting our hair down. Even the most staid Christians eventually thawed out and enjoyed the fun. We rounded off the evening with an enormous spread of food prepared by my wife and other wives. Diets went by the board and we tucked into a multitude of appetizing dishes. A simple epilogue and a few carols brought the occasion to an appropriate conclusion and the guests went home tired but happy! This may seem a strange kind of pastoral work but at least our visitors knew that we were quite normal and able to see the funny side of life. It is amazing how such an event as this helps to give people confidence in us, and the following weeks brought many useful contacts and personal conversations.

One thing which we began to realise as time went on was that much of what people told us was in strictest confidence and often had never been said before to anyone. Many times I even felt that it would be wrong to tell my wife some of of the things I had been told and I believe that each of us should be most careful not to repeat what has been mentioned confidentially. There are many occasions on which we mention things as matters for prayer, whereas in reality this is merely a cover-up for the fact that we are gossiping.

Although the emphasis in this chapter has been very

much on the physical side of pastoral help, ultimately we must influence our group members spiritually. Apart from talking about the Scriptures, etc., in their homes and in our own home, one of the most effective ways of helping was by lending Christian books to group members. Missionary books especially brought great blessing to many who read them. Over the years we had accumulated many books about the lives of devoted Christians and we ourselves had been challenged by them. We suggested to one or two members that they should do some Christian reading and offered them a selection of books by such authors as Isabel Kuhn. Soon they were back for more, and others, too, became enthusiastic about reading such books, so much so that I had to keep a record of books and who had them, rather like a miniature library. Some were such avid readers that we found it difficult to satisfy their appetite, and we had to make frequent visits to the Christian bookshop to buy the latest books.

You may doubt the value of such a ministry of lending books since it does not directly relate to a study and meditation of the Bible. But we noticed that reading the accounts of how God led these great Christian missionaries through such trials into glorious victories for Him caused the readers to seek a deeper relationship to the Lord. It also enlarged their vision for Him and helped build up greater confidence in God's mighty power. It directed them to the Scriptures which so frequently were quoted by the authors and had so influenced their lives.

One couple in particular used to spend a while each night reading novels before retiring to bed. As they began to read about God's work, their interest in the novels gradually disappeared as they found spiritual nourishment in the biographies of God's servants. The husband eventually felt the need for deeper reading and began to study the great Christian doctrines and spend more and more time in the Scriptures.

In all our Christian activity and pastoral care we should never lose sight of the fact that blessing can come only direct from God through the Holy Spirit. Humanly speaking we do all we can for our Lord yet knowing that we are simply channels of blessing. Pastoral care may seem arduous and at times unrewarding yet I believe it is what God wants us to do as our responsibility in working for Him. We sow the seed, which is the precious Word of God, yet we show the love of God by our genuine love and attention.

Seven

Conclusion

IN THE EARLIER CHAPTERS OF THIS BOOK WE HAVE TRIED TO explain something of what is involved in home Bible studies. Much of the advice you will already have had but perhaps the suggestions drawn from our own experiences may be of help. Some of the methods and ideas are no doubt rather unusual and unorthodox, but we trust that you will prayerfully consider some of the details before rejecting them. The obvious benefits of such studies are to be found in the lives of those whose hearts have been opened by the Lord as a result of studying the Scriptures in an organised fashion.

In writing these things, we do not wish to imply in any way that God is not blessing other methods of reading and studying the Bible. Bible studies are not intended to replace private meditation on God's Word or to become a substitute for working in our own Churches and hearing God's Word expounded from the pulpit. The Holy Spirit can use the Scriptures, no matter what the circumstances in which they are read.

However, the effectiveness of being amongst others and hearing them read and discuss passages of Scripture cannot be questioned. There is nothing more helpful than to sit in someone's living-room listening to Christians telling their experiences in the Christian life, explaining the Scriptures they have found helpful and describing the lessons they have learned. Discussing the Bible in this relaxed way can enrich our Christian lives, giving us greater confidence in our Saviour and a fuller realization of His love and care for us. And a Christian home which has been dedicated to the Lord can help an unbeliever to see the reality of the Christian faith in the lives of those Christians.

The process of digging out the answers from the Bible and then applying them to our lives has brought great reward in my own life and in the lives of many others who have studied the Scriptures in this way. For many it has been the means of finding God's help with their personal problems and for some it has been the means of finding the strength and ability to help others discover God's answers.

For example there were John and Dorothy, a middle-aged couple, who were converted about eight years ago, but although they trusted in the Lord, they were without great joy or purpose. Their knowledge of the Bible was very slight, apart from verses which spoke about their salvation. They went from church to church in order to find greater help and joy, and yet they never felt that they had learned much by listening to pulpit ministry. They began to attend a home bible study, but were hesitant and said very little for several weeks. Slowly they started understanding the Scriptures and finding their way around in their Bibles. We saw them slowly blossom, learning to apply the help they received from the Bible, realising their responsibility in a local church, reading a wide selection of Christian literature and witnessing to others about Jesus Christ. As John became more confident he led one or two Bible studies, and eventually was given the responsibility of organising regular Bible studies for his church. As time went on he saw the unhappiness of the people living near him and God gave him a deep longing to tell them about Christ. He began witnessing from door to door and before long there was one more family regularly attending his church, eagerly listening to the message of life in Christ.

To imply that the method we used in Bible studies was

the reason for the changed lives and growth in grace would be presumptuous. It was the Holy Spirit using the Scriptures and making the truth effectual which brought blessing, but on the human level, the method used helped to make understanding the Bible that bit easier for all those who came.

APPENDIX OF USEFUL STUDIES

THE FOLLOWING NOTES vary from the simple to the more advanced, to cater for Bible study groups of differing spiritual maturity. The variations are by no means absolute, and the group leader should choose studies to suit his own group. Since the construction and preparation of Bible studies has been dealt with in Ch. 4, these notes are intended only as a guide and do not necessarily lend themselves to use exactly as they stand. For example, the readings are not exhaustive, and more suitable ones may be found relating to the different topics studied. The leader may also wish to amplify the Introduction by using commentaries and suggestions of his own. Some groups may prefer to discuss the topics or passages without the use of the questions, though the leader could bear them in mind as the discussion proceeds and use them if he feels the need. In any case, there are many more questions which the leader could raise which are not included here.

THE WORLD IN NEED

Readings Matthew 9: 1-8. 11: 28-30. John 14: 6

Introduction

As we look around us in the world we can all see the obvious physical needs caused by war, overpopulation, famine and disease. The spiritual needs though less obvious have a widespread and devastating effect upon the human race. Doctors maintain that many of their patients are spiritually sick even though their symptoms seem to be caused by physical illness. The real needs of individuals today can be seen from the increase of boredom, unhappiness, loneliness, frustration, lack of purpose and many other things, in spite of material advantages.

Jesus Christ claimed to be the answer to human need in His day and the Bible tells us that He continues to be even today. Christians need to be convinced of this in order to benefit themselves and pass it on to others. Those seeking a real faith and purpose in life should examine for themselves the claims of Christ by reading their Bibles.

In our first reading we see that the palsied man's real need was a spiritual one, the forgiveness of sins, not just a desire to be cured of his disease. In the next passage Jesus claims to be able and willing to take our burdens upon Himself, and in John's gospel 14: 6 he says He is our way, truth and life, that is the answer to our deepest needs for direction of life, a real standard of truth and the source of real life.

Questions:

1. Why was the forgiveness of sins so important to the palsied man, and of what importance is this to me?

2. What are the real burdens which we carry about with us?

3. In what ways will Jesus be able to bear my burdens?

4. How can I be sure that Jesus's claims are true?

5. Why is it better to entrust the direction of my life to Christ rather than to determine it myself?

6. Surely truth is a matter of opinion, so why does it matter that Jesus claims to represent real truth?

7. Jesus claimed to be life and to bring life but how is this different from everyday life?

THE NECESSITY OF THE CROSS

Readings Numbers 21: 5-9. John 3: 14-18

Introduction

Each one of us, before we commit our lives to Christ, is under condemnation before God. We are guilty of not living up to God's standards (Romans 3: 23) and have broken God's commandments. For these transgressions we deserve punishment and especially for not yet having received Christ as our Saviour and Lord. The Bible says that although we are living in a human sense, we do not have eternal life, which can come only from God, by receiving Christ into our lives.

John describes our condition as being like that of the Israelites in the wilderness who had been bitten by a serpent. Their only remedy was to look up at the brass serpent on a pole, which instantly prevented their death. When Jesus was crucified He too was lifted up just like the brass serpent. "The Cross" is the name given to the death of Christ when He died to give life to those who would turn to Him for forgiveness of their sins and freedom from condemnation. Just as the Israelites could not cure themselves of their serpent bites, no one can receive eternal life without turning to Christ, whose death was a necessity as far as we are concerned, because only in this way could He bear the punishment of our sins and take away the condemnation.

Questions:

1. Why was God so displeased with the Israelites that they had to be punished?
2. Is there anything in our lives for which we deserve God's anger?
3. Why do you think Jesus was willing to die for us?
4. Is there any way of being freed from condemnation other than by trusting Christ?

5. Does offering my life to Christ automatically bring forgiveness of sins and eternal life or do I have to do something more?

6. What is it like to possess eternal life?

WHAT IS A CHRISTIAN?

Readings Acts 16: 22-34. Ephesians 2: 8-9

Introduction

In spite of the common usage of the word "Christian" today, there are only three references to it in the entire New Testament (Acts 26:28, 11:26, I Peter 4:16). It seems to have been used first as a nickname and then adopted by the believers themselves. Today its meaning is rather vague and has even degenerated into an adjective in such phrases as "it's the Christian thing to do." In England we often refer to a person as a Christian if they fulfil certain requirements such as being baptised in the Church, confirmed and married in the Church, doing good to neighbours, saying prayers, attending Church etc. Many people feel today that in England it is unnecessary to emphasise the fact of becoming a Christian since this is the accepted religion of our country.

Questions:

1. In Acts 16: 30 the jailor wanted to be saved. Did he want to be saved merely from punishment by the Romans or from something else?

2. After he had become a Christian, the jailor was overjoyed. Have we ever known a time when we knew such a joy as his?

3. Becoming a Christian is often called Conversion— just what does this involve?

4. Many people feel that by doing good works they can

merit God's favour. What else is involved besides good works?

5. How can I personally have faith?

THE BIBLE IN MY LIFE

Readings I Peter 1: 23-2: 3. II Tim. 3: 16, 17.
Ps. 119: 7-11

Introduction

In Peter's epistle we are told that it was the Bible which caused the Christians to respond to the gospel message. He also informs his readers that those who are young in the faith (called newborn babes in verse 2) should desire to feed upon the Scriptures.

Paul tells Timothy that the entire Bible is inspired by God (literally God-breathed) and is vital to the daily life of a Christian as our teacher, corrector, and instructor in what is right.

In Psalm 119 the author describes the secret of clean-living as obedience to God's Word. He also says that a conscious storing-up of the Bible in my life and experience will help prevent committing many sins.

Questions:

1. How is it that the Bible is so powerful that it can persuade people to commit their lives to Christ?

2. What happens to us if we neglect the Bible?

3. Why is it so important that the Bible is truly inspired?

4. How should we study the Bible in order to be fully equipped Christians?

5. How does the Bible prevent us from falling into sin?

GUIDANCE

Readings Phil. 2: 13. John 14: 13, 14, 21. Ps. 119: 105

Introduction

Oliver Barclay has said: "The only safe way of obtaining guidance is to keep strictly to Biblical principles." Not only is it essential for a happy Christian life to allow God to guide us but we are commanded in Eph. 5: 17 to understand what the will of the Lord is. We must remember that God has committed Himself to guiding us. (e.g. Ps. 32: 8) all we have to do is to discern in which direction God is telling us to go.

In Phil. 2: 13 we are told that God, through the Holy Spirit, works in us in order to reveal His will for us but at the same time we are responsible to pray to God, as John 14: 13, 14 tells us. Also, we must turn to the Bible for guidance about many things as that well known verse Ps. 119: 105 instructs us.

Many of us make our own plans for the future and then ask God to add His blessing, but it is much better to let God work things out in His own way. It is also possible to deliberately go against God's revealed will due to our own stubbornness. Looking back to how God led us in the past is often easier than waiting for Him to lead us in the future.

Questions:

1. If God is at work in me through the Spirit revealing His will to me why can I simply not rely on my feelings and be guided by them?

2. John 14: 14 seems to suggest that whatever I want I can have by merely asking for it. Is it so simple as this or is there more to it?

3. Since the Bible doesn't give specific details about everything on which I need guidance (for example, which job to take) how can I use it as my guide?

4. Why should I allow God to guide me? Can't I lead my own life the way I want to?

PRAYER

Readings John 2: 1-11. I John 3: 19-24

Introduction

To pray is "to open the door of our hearts, to give Jesus access to our needs, to allow Him to exercise His own power in dealing with them." In the story of the miracle at Cana of Galilee we have an example of effective prayer. When we pray it should be in an attitude of helplessness and yet faith that believes that God will answer. There are several kinds of prayer—supplicatory (request), thanksgiving, praise for what God is, and prayers without words.

Two kinds of Christians are described in John's epistle —those who are not walking closely to the Lord (v. 20) and others whose lives are pleasing to God and in Whose presence they feel completely relaxed (v. 21). We are told here that the latter kind of Christian has the privilege of God saying "Yes" to their prayers.

Questions:

1. In John 15: 5 Jesus said "Without Me ye can do nothing." In our prayer life to what extent should we take this literally?

2. How can I have enough faith to be sure that God will answer my prayers?

3. Can you draw examples of the right ways to pray from the passage in John's Gospel?

4. Why does it hinder our prayer-life if we fail to please God in our lives?

5. Verse 22 of I John 3 suggests that God will give us absolutely anything we ask for, but what kind of restrictions are there on what is valid in our prayer requests?

THE CHRISTIAN IN A MODERN WORLD

Readings I John 2: 15-17. Luke 5: 27-30.
2 Cor. 5: 18-20

Introduction

The subject of worldliness has been debated by Christians since the Lord was on earth. Some have taken up monasticism in order to be free from the world, others have indulged in every kind of activity possible in order to be in touch with people. The Christian is said to be "in" the world but not "of" the world, and there must be a middle path in which one can be separate from evil yet in a position to reach people for Christ. Jesus Himself of course is the supreme example of balance between the two extremes. In His dealings with sinners such as Matthew and his friends the Lord was in contact yet separate from their evil. 2 Cor. 5:20 says that we are ambassadors for Christ, that is His earthly representatives and as such we do have to be in the company of earthly people rather than isolated in a monastery.

Questions:

1. Why were the Scribes and Pharisees critical of the Lord's association with Matthew and his friends?

2. In John 3: 16 we are told that God loved the world, yet in I John 2: 15 we are instructed not to love the world—how can this be?

3. I John 2: 16 says that we must not involve ourselves in the lust of the flesh, the lust of the eyes and the pride of life. What kind of things come under these general headings of things that I shouldn't do?

4. If it is wrong to love the world, then how can I truly represent Christ is seeking to win people for Him without compromising myself? Can we think of ways in which we can legitimately rub shoulders with non-Christians?

SHOULD WE WORRY?

Readings Mark 4: 37-41. Matt. 6: 25-34. Phil. 4: 6, 7

Introduction

In the story of the calming of the storm we have a good example of what worry is all about. In verse 38 the disciples had no confidence that Jesus would prevent them from drowning. Basically, worry might be thought of as a lack of confidence that God is in control of every situation. It is very surprising that they had so little faith in the One who was the mighty Creator.

In the passage from the Sermon on the Mount (Matt. 6) the Lord turns our attention from ourselves and our problems to the world of nature. In that sphere it is God Himself who provides directly for the welfare of flowers and plants, none of which consciously have to work to be maintained. Provided we put God first there is the promise that we need not be anxious about our present day needs (v. 33) or those of the future (v. 34).

In Paul's letter to the Philippians there is a clear command not to be anxious but to commit our problems to God in prayer. God then promises to bring real peace into our hearts and minds.

Questions:

1. Why did Jesus allow the storm to be so violent that they thought He had forsaken them?

2. How do we react when things really go wrong?

3. In Matt. 6: 25 and 34 the disciples are told to take no thought about material things, but does it mean this literally?

4. How can I be sure of provision for my needs if I do seek first the Kingdom of God.

5. Have any of us ever tried telling God about our problems and did we really experience inner peace?

HOW GOD DEALS WITH EACH OF US IN THE NEXT LIFE

Readings Revelation 20: 4-6 and 11-15. I Cor. 3: 11-15

Introduction

As far as a Christian is concerned the next major event in God's calendar is the return of Christ from heaven when He will remove all Christians to heaven. Those who are alive at that time will have their earthly bodies instantly transformed into resurrection bodies and those who have died will be raised from the dead, again receiving eternal resurrection bodies. After a period of turmoil on earth, Christ will return as the King of all the earth, and together with all the Christians who accompany Him will exercise His rule over the earth for a thousand years. This is described in the last part of Rev. 20: 4 and 6. Those who reject Christ as Saviour will not take part in this first resurrection (Rev. 20: 5) but will be resurrected at the end of the thousand years and brought before the Great White Throne where God will condemn them. See Rev. 20: 11-15.

Although the passage in I Cor. 3 refers to the Christian ministry, we may apply it to all our service on earth for God. Jesus Christ is the foundation for all that we do (v. 11). What each of us does in our lives is represented by those things of value, gold, silver, precious stones or those things like wood, hay, stubble which have relatively little value. Each of us in the next life will be assessed by Christ as to the value of our service. It will be as if all our works were subjected to fire when only the good things will remain. Our rewards will be varied according to what is of value, and the Bible indicates that when we assist Christ as King the amount of responsibility given to us will be determined by our good works in this life. Some of us, alas, will get no reward (v. 15) though of course, we cannot lose our salvation and a place in heaven.

Questions:

1. What do you think it will be like on earth after Christ has removed all the Christians by taking them to heaven?

2. Why will it be necessary for God to condemn all those who rejected Christ in their lifetime?

3. How can we be sure that our work for God is built on the right foundation?

4. How is it possible for a Christian to do good works which are of no value?

5. If all my works turn out to be of no value when Christ assesses them, how can I be sure of not losing my place in heaven?

WHAT IS THE REAL CHURCH?

Readings Matthew 16: 15-18. I Cor. 12: 12-24

Introduction

As soon as Peter realised that the man called Jesus was actually God's Son and was the promised Messiah, Jesus told him how the Church would be founded. Its basis was to be the declaration that the historical Jesus was in fact God's Son, the Messiah, and that those who recognised the identity of Jesus would belong to the real Church.

In the verses from I Corinthians the Church is portrayed as a body having a head (Christ, of course) and all the other parts that make up a normal body (these representing the Christians). Every Christian has a particular function within the Church just as the various parts of our body have a vital part to play in daily living. In spite of these differences in function, no Christian can despise his fellow believer because each one of us although different is a useful member of the body.

Questions:

1. Some people think that the Church is founded on Peter, why can this not be so?
2. In order to belong to the real Church is it necessary to do more than intellectually agree that Jesus is God's Son?
3. Why is Christ's relationship to His Church compared with the body and head of a human being?
4. Why has God given each of us a different function and position in the Church?
5. Am I personally aware of the task God has given me to do in the Church or in my local Church.

THE HOLY SPIRIT

Readings   Ephesians 1: 13, 14. I Cor. 6: 19-20.
                John 16: 13-15

Introduction

Many people are confused as to who or what the Holy Spirit is, Christianity has one God yet God is three Persons, God the Father, God the Son and God the Holy Spirit. So He is the third Person of the Godhead, not a mere influence. It took the early Church quite a long time to realise that He was just as much God as was the Father and the Son. On several occasions in the New Testament we find the three Persons closely grouped together such as in the commands concerning baptism where it is done in the name of the Father, Son and Spirit.

Paul tells us in Ephesians that a Christian is sealed by the Holy Spirit, who is really a kind of down-payment ("earnest" in Eph. 1: 14) by God to us, the rest of the blessing coming in the next life. In I Corinthians Paul says that the Holy Spirit actually lives inside the body of each Christian and that since Christ really bought us when He died for us then we should be honouring to Him in our lives. John says that the task of the Holy Spirit is to enable us to understand what is the truth about Christianity. His prime purpose is to help us to see how wonderful a person Jesus is.

Questions:
1. Under what circumstances does God send the Holy Spirit to indwell us?
2. How can I be sure that God will never forsake me?
3. Since the Holy Spirit lives in my body and I now belong to Christ, how should this affect my way of living?
4. Why does the Holy Spirit not magnify and glorify Himself?
5. Since the Holy Spirit can guide us into all the truth, does this mean that I have no responsibility in the matter at all?
6. How can I effectively ensure that the Holy Spirit performs His desired work in me?

THE MEANING OF THE RESURRECTION

Readings I Cor. 15: 12-19. John 7: 37-39

Introduction

It is surprising how many people accept as facts the details of ancient history about which there is very little known. Yet the same people find it hard to believe that Christ actually rose from the dead in spite of the large amount of available evidence both from the Bible and historical writings. The greatest testimony of course comes from the lives of Christians who know that Jesus is alive today and have a relationship to Him.

1 Cor. 15:3-8 presents the evidence for the resurrection. In vv. 12-19 Paul shows that if Christ did not rise then none of us could be sure that our sins had been forgiven or that those Christians who have died will ever attain heaven. In

fact Paul concludes by saying that if we have given our lives to a dead Saviour then we are to be pitied!

In John 7, Jesus said that after He was glorified those who believed on Him would receive the Holy Spirit. Naturally, without the resurrection no one could have been given the Holy Spirit.

Questions:

1. In I Cor. 15: 14 Paul says that our faith is in vain if Christ had not risen. Why would it not suffice to follow just the teachings and example of Jesus as in other religions?
2. What is the connexion between the resurrection and the forgiveness of our sins.
3. Why is there no guarantee that Christians who have died are in heaven if Christ did not rise?
4. Of what importance is it that each of us receives the Holy Spirit when we believe on Christ?

JOYFUL LIVING—STUDIES IN PHILIPPIANS

1. The Christian's triumph in the face of suffering.   1:1-30
2. The life of Christ—an example for us.   2:1-11
3. Working out my Christian life.   2:12-30
4. Putting Christ first.   3:1-21
5. Joy and peace.   4:1-9
6. Learning to be content.   4:10-23

THE CHRISTIAN'S TRIUMPH IN THE FACE OF SUFFERING

Reading Phil. 1: 1-30

Introduction

The first European Church was that founded by Paul at Philippi a Roman colony in Macedonia. Acts 16: 12-40 tells us of Paul's activities. This letter to the Church was written by Paul from prison, probably in Rome about A.D. 64. There are three main reasons why he wrote to them:—

    i. To thank them for their gift of money.

    ii. To request that they should be unified.

    iii. To encourage them to rejoice.

In vv. 1-11 Paul relates his happy memories of that Church and longs to see them again.

vv. 12-19 explain why he can be joyful even while suffering. Because of his imprisonment the good news of Jesus Christ had spread widely.

From vv. 20-26 Paul talks about himself. He is prepared to die for the sake of Christ, though willing to remain alive for the sake of the Philippians.

Finally, he exhorts them to practice what they preach and to be courageous in the face of opposition because it is to be expected in the Christian life.

Questions:

1. Why does Paul think of the Philippians with such affection?
2. In what way do we think of our fellow Christians?
3. How had Paul's suffering caused the spread of the gospel?
4. Does our suffering always result in exalting Christ?
5. Paul was prepared to live or die according to God's will. How willing are we to do what God wants?
6. Why is it important to practise what we preach?

THE LIFE OF CHRIST AN EXAMPLE FOR US

Reading Phil. 2: 1-11

Introduction

  In vv. 1-4 Paul exhorts the Christians to three things

    i. Oneness v. 2

   ii. Lowliness v. 3

   iii. Helpfulness v. 4

"If" in v. 1 really means "since" and here there are four reasons for the above exhortations:

   i. Consolation in Christ=Paul's authority to exhort comes from Christ.

   ii. Comfort of love=control of love. Christ's love controls us=2 Cor. 5: 14.

   iii. Fellowship of the Spirit=all have corporate life in the Spirit.

   iv. Bowels and mercies=affectionate sympathy of Christ for them and for each other.

The fulfilment of the above exhortations is found in Christ whose qualities and life Paul describes in vv. 6-8. Here there are some difficult expressions which need explaining.

v. 6 means that Christ, although God, did not insist on displaying His divine glories while a man on earth.

v. 7. In becoming a servant He was not play acting as the word "form" suggests but was a real human being.

His greatest act of love for others was His death on the cross.

In vv. 9-11 we see how God took the initiative in exalting Christ in every possible way both then, now and in the future.

Questions:

1. Of what importance to a Christian Church is it that we each should be united, lowly and helpful?

2. To what extent are we individually controlled by Christ's love and how should this affect my attitude to others?

3. It is a fact that we each possess the same Holy Spirit, but how does this fact help to unify Christians?

4. In what ways did Christ not show His true Divine splendour?

5. What caused Christ to humble Himself to the extent that He died on the Cross?

6. Why has God been able to exalt Christ to such a high position and how should this affect us?

WORKING OUT MY CHRISTIAN LIFE

Reading Phil. 2: 12-30.

Introduction

Having shown Christ to be the supreme example of dedication o God's will (vv. 5-8), Paul now exhorts the Philippians to be obedient to God's revealed will. Such obedience would result in their lives being pleasing to God (vv. 12-13), good relationships within their church (v. 14), and a bright testimony in the world outside (v. 16).

In vv. 19-24 Timothy is commended as one who has already proved himself and is eminently qualified to care for the Christians.

Epaphroditus (meaning "charming") had already been sent back to the Philippians by Paul (v. 25) because they were anxious about his health, and Paul here reminds them that he almost died as a result of serving Christ (v. 30).

Questions:

1. In what sense does Paul exhort the Philippians to work out their own salvation?

2. How should the promises in v. 13 affect my Christian life?

3. In what ways should my life be contrasted with the dark world in which I live?

4. How can I become qualified to receive such a commendation as Timothy received from Paul?

5. To what extent should we allow our health to suffer for the sake of God's work?

PUTTING CHRIST FIRST

Reading Phil. 3: 1-21

Introduction

In vv. 1-3 Paul warns the Philippians against any Judaisers who may attempt to introduce legalistic practices and principles into the church.

Although Paul possessed many qualifications which would make any other man boastful (vv. 4-6), his only desire is to know Christ and for him this involves regarding his human attainments as worthless (vv. 7-9). Paul's desire to know Christ as an all-sufficient Saviour causes him to be willing to even die for Christ (vv. 10, 11).

Although Paul had already attained great spiritual stature, he was humble enough to recognise that even he had not yet attained the degree of maturity to which God was leading him (vv. 12-16).

Questions:

1. What danger is there in allowing legalism to creep into our Christian churches?
2. Is Paul implying in this passage that it is wrong for a Christian to receive training and education?
3. How can I put into practice my desire to know Christ better?
4. What steps can I take to become a more mature Christian?
5. Is it possible to attain sinless perfection in this life?

JOY AND PEACE

Reading Phil. 4: 1-9

Introduction

In the athletic games of the first century the reward presented to those who were victorious was a garland of leaves called a crown (Greek stephanos). Paul was so delighted with the believers at Philippi that he regarded them as his reward for his Christian service (v. 1).

The words "shall keep" in v. 7 are from a military word "shall mount guard." God's peace, like a sentinel, mounts guard and patrols before the heart's door, keeping worry out.

In v. 8 the expression "think on these things" is much deeper than it appears, and implies that we must both take into account and act upon the things Paul has mentioned.

Questions:

1. What are the causes of quarelling in the local church?
2. What should each of us do to make sure that we are "of the same mind in the Lord"? (v. 2)
3. For what reasons does a Christian rejoice and should this depend on our circumstances? (v. 4)
4. Does v. 6 imply that a Christian should take a couldn't care less attitude?
5. What practical steps should each of us take to obey Paul's commands in v. 8?

LEARNING TO BE CONTENT

Reading Phil. 4: 10-23

Introduction

Although Paul rejoiced in the fact that his financial support had finally arrived (v. 10) it is clear that his inner peace did not depend on his outward circumstances which had been anything but peaceful (vv. 11-13). We can see that Paul's desire for a gift was not a selfish one in that he really wanted the givers to receive a blessing (v. 17). He also pointed out in v. 18 that giving was a form of worship which was pleasing to God. In any case those who give of their substance need not fear poverty as God would supply their needs too (v. 19).

Questions:

1. Are we content to accept the circumstances in which God has placed us or does our inner peace fluctuate depending on whether things go badly or well?
2. What is the secret of remaining continually joyful?
3. How do we know that Christ will look after us materially as well as spiritually?
4. What kind of benefits are there for those who give generously to the Lord?
5. We usually think of worship as being associated with church services and meditation. How can Christian service be regarded as worship?
6. If I am generous in my giving of time and money to God how can I be sure that He will not let me suffer for it?

BOOK LIST

THERE ARE about 100 individual titles here, which for practical reasons have been listed under the following headings:

1. The Christian Home as a Centre for Witness.
2. Bible Study Material.
3. Bible Commentaries Suitable for Preparing Bible Studies.
4. Books for Lending or Giving.
5. Books for Personal Libraries.

1. The Christian Home as a Centre for Witness

How have other Christians used their homes for God? These stimulating stories should encourage every reader to examine the possibilities of becoming personally involved in Home Evangelism.

Miller, Keith, *A Taste of New Wine* (Word Books).
              A Second Touch (Word Books).
Warde, Margaret, *Take My Home* (S.U.).
Rees, Tom, *Breakthrough* (Hildenborough Bookroom).
Batchelor, Mary, *Within these Four Walls* (S.U.).
Capenerhurst, R., *You in your Small Corner* (I.V.P.).

2. Bible Study Material

Most authors have concentrated their efforts on young people's Bible Studies, but with a little ingenuity the literature available may be adapted to adult work. The 3 books below are concerned with the techniques involved in running Home Bible Studies, the most systematic one being the first.

Cotterill, J. H., and Hews, M., *Know How to Lead Bible Study and Discussion Groups* (S.U.). For Young People.

Leading the Bible Study Group (S.U.). Small Booklet.

Rees, Tom, *Breakthrough*, (Hildenborough Bookroom).

The following notes may be used in the Study itself without causing much additional work by the leader of the group.

Stibbs, Alan, *Search the Scriptures* (I.V.P.). Suggestions for study from the entire Bible, designed for students; may be too difficult for some groups.

Adult Teacher (Scripture Press). Sold by some Christian bookshops, also from 372 Caledonian Rd., London N1.

Studies in Christian Living (The Navigators). These booklets have spaces for written answers and are helpful for either personal or group study. A series of 10 obtainable from some bookshops, or from 89A The Broadway, Wimbledon, London SW 29.

Notes from Lansdowne Bible School. Printed notes of Bible studies conducted by Rev. Francis W. Dixon. Used by many groups. Tapes also available. Apply to Lansdowne Baptist Church, Bournemouth.

3. Bible Commentaries Suitable for Preparing Bible Studies

Commentaries provide a useful source of background information as well as being an aid to understanding the Bible narrative.

Mears, Henrietta C., *What the Bible is all about* (Gospel Light). Simple approach, but much useful material.

Matthew Henry Commentary (M.M.S.). Devotional style.

New Bible Commentary (*Revised*) (I.V.P.). Good background material.

Each of these works covers the whole Bible.

Several publishers have issued series of books on Bible exposition:

Tyndale New Testament Commentaries (I.V.P.). Detailed exposition of every book.

Tyndale Old Testament Commentaries (I.V.P.). Genesis, Proverbs, Ezekiel, Judges and Ruth; others to follow.

Bible Study Books (S.U.). More general comments on passages of Scripture throughout whole Bible, some now out of print.

Everymans Bible Commentaries (Moody Press). Devotional, on most books of N.T. and some of O.T.).

Emmaus Correspondence Courses. Apply to 102 Eastham Rake, Eastham, Wirral, Cheshire. Devotional and practical with some fairly easy questions in each chapter.

The remaining books on various portions of the Bible are not exhaustive but may provide guidance in Bible Study preparation.

Redpath, Alan, *Victorious Christian Living* (P. & I.). (Joshua).

The Making of a Man of God (P. & I.). (David).

Victorious Christian Service (P. & I.). (Nehemiah).

Lloyd-Jones, D. M., *Sermon on the Mount* (I.V.P.). (Matthew 5-7).

Stott, J. R. W., *Men Made New* (I.V.P.). (Romans 5-8).

Galatians (I.V.P.).

Nee, Watchman, *Sit Walk Stand* (Victory Press). (Ephesians).

For studies in Doctrine it is helpful to have a copy of a book which deals specifically with the major Christian doctrines.

Berkhof, L., *Systematic Theology* (Banner of Truth). Very comprehensive.

Hammond, T. C., *In Understanding be Men* (I.V.P.).

A concordance is a necessity for Bible Study preparation, the choice being determined by the depth to which the leader intends to go.

Cruden's Concordance (Lutterworth). Good for finding texts.

Young's Concordance (Lutterworth). Useful for those needing Greek words as well as locating verses.

Strong's Concordance (Hodder). Probably the best—fully comprehensive.

4. Books for lending or giving

Missionary books have been instrumental in the conversion of many people. Christians too have been revitalised by reading stories of courageous Christians on the mission field.

Kuhn, Isobel, *By Searching* (O.M.F.).
    In the Arena (O.M.F.).
    Ascent to the Tribes (O.M.F.).
    Precious things of the Lasting Hills (O.M.F.).
    Nests above the Abyss (O.M.F.).
    Stones of Fire (O.M.F.).
    Green leaf in Drought (O.M.F.).

Canfield, Carolyn L., *One Vision only* (O.M.F.). Biography of Isobel Kuhn.

Broomhall, Marshall, *The Man Who believed God*. O.M.F. Biography of Hudson Taylor.

Elliott, Elizabeth,
    Through Gates of Splendour (Hodder). ⎱ Stories about five missionaries murdered in Ecuador.
    Shadow of the Almighty (Hodder).
Hitt, Russell T., *Jungle Pilot* (Hodder).

Bull, G. T., *When Iron Gates Yield* (Hodder). A British missionary held captive by Chinese communists for 3 years.
    God Holds the Key (Hodder).
    Tibetan Tales (Hodder).
    Coral in the Sand (Hodder). North Borneo.

Popov, Haralan, *Tortured for His Faith* (M.M.S.). Bulgarian Pastor imprisoned 13 years by Communists.

Wurmbrand, R., *The Soviet Saints* (Hodder).
    In God's Underground (Hodder).
    Tortured for Christ (Hodder).
    If that were Christ would you give Him your blanket? (Hodder).

Wilson, Dorothy C.,
    Ten Fingers for God (Hodder). ⎱ Medical missionary work in India.
    Take my Hands (Hodder).

Hayes, M., *Missing, Believed Killed* (Hodder). Congo.

Roseveare, Helen, *Give me This Mountain* (I.V.P.). Congo.

Hunter, Christine, *Gladys Aylward* (Coverdale). China.

Andrew, Brother, *God's Smuggler* (Hodder). A Dutch Christian who penetrates communist countries with Bibles.

Houghton, Frank, *Amy Carmichael of Dohnavur* (S.P.C.K.). A biography . S.P.C.K. also publish books and poems by Amy Carmichael.

Garton, Nancy, *George Muller* (Hodder).

Schaeffer, Edith, *L'Abri* (Norfolk Press). Work in a Christian centre in Switzerland.

For those whose appetites for reading have been stimulated by missionary books, there are more general ones which we may recommend to them.

Nee, Watchman, *The Normal Christian Life* (Victory Press).

Lloyd-Jones, D. M., *Spiritual Depression* (P. & I.).

Hallesby, O., *Prayer* (I.V.P.).

Dempster, G. F., *The Love that Will not
          Let Me Go* (Hodder).   ⎱ Stories
     Touched by a Loving Hand   ⎰ of men
     Finding Men for Christ   ⎱ and women
     Lovest Thou Me ?   ⎰ found for
     Until He finds It.   Christ.

A Christian's Guide to . . . (Hodder). Series containing such titles as "Discovering God's will", "Prayer" etc.

Blanchard, John, *Right with God* (Banner of Truth).

A number of authors have written books especially for women:

Price, Eugenia, *The Burden is Light* (Oliphants). Autobiography.
          Woman to Woman (Oliphants).
          Make Love your Aim (Oliphants).

Ashton, Marion L., *A Mind at Ease* (Overcomer Bookroom).
          The Lord Between For Ever. Published by Dr. Ashton.
          The Way of Peace in the Midst of Tension Published by Dr. Ashton.

Fowke, Ruth, *Coping with Crises* (Hodder).

Schaeffer, Edith, *Hidden Art* (Norfolk Press). Recognising that even the mundane things can be worthwhile.

5. Books for Personal Libraries

Many of the books already mentioned should find a place on all our bookshelves. For example, we all need to use commentaries, concordances and works on doctrine, as well as many of the books in section 4. The remaining ones listed here will add depth and breadth to our reading, although they represent only a small fraction of all the excellent books now on sale.

Little, Paul E., *How to Give Away your Faith* (I.V.P.). A stimulating if not radical approach to personal evangelism.

Smith, Ron, *The A.B.C. of Personal Evangelism* (The Fishers Fellowship, 96 Plaistow Lane, Bromley, Kent).

Griffiths, Michael, *Give Up Your Small Ambitions* (I.V.P.). A practical approach to full-time service.

Broomhall, A. J., *A Time for Action* (I.V.P.). A challenge to more active service.

Capenerhurst, R. and Stride, E., *God at Ground Level* (Falcon). Christianity in action on the factory floor.

Stott, J. R. W., *Basic Christianity* (I.V.P.).

Hopkins, H. E., *Henceforth* (I.V.P.). Christian dedication.

Catherwood, H. F. R., *The Christian Citizen* (Hodder).

Green, Michael, *Choose Freedom* (I.V.P.). Jesus Christ the answer to personal freedom.

Rinker, Rosalind, *Prayer, Conversing with God.* (Zondervan).

Sanders, J. O., *Heresies and Cults* (Oliphants).

Ridenour, Fritz, *So What's The Difference?* (Gospel Light).